T0090391

INVEST IN COSTA RICA

Easy, Fast & Secure.

A simple guide to understanding the real estate system and buying process in Costa Rica, with legal advise and tips to make your experience straightforward and profitable.

By

NICHOLAS P. VIALE

Order this book online at www.trafford.com
or email orders@trafford.com

Most Trafford titles are also available at major online book retailers.

Note for Librarians: A cataloguing record for this book is available from Library and Archives Canada at www.collectionscanada.ca/amicus/index-e.html

Printed in Victoria, BC, Canada.

ISBN: 978-1-4251-6355-6 (Soft)
ISBN: 978-1-4251-6369-3 (e-book)

We at Trafford believe that it is the responsibility of us all, as both individuals and corporations, to make choices that are environmentally and socially sound. You, in turn, are supporting this responsible conduct each time you purchase a Trafford book, or make use of our publishing services. To find out how you are helping, please visit www.trafford.com/responsiblepublishing.html

Our mission is to efficiently provide the world's finest, most comprehensive book publishing service, enabling every author to experience success. To find out how to publish your book, your way, and have it available worldwide, visit us online at www.trafford.com

Trafford rev. 6/22/2009

Trafford PUBLISHING® www.trafford.com

North America & international
toll-free: 1 888 232 4444 (USA & Canada)
phone: 250 383 6864 ♦ fax: 250 383 6804 ♦ email: info@trafford.com

The United Kingdom & Europe
phone: +44 (0)1865 487 395 ♦ local rate: 0845 230 9601
facsimile: +44 (0)1865 481 507 ♦ email: info.uk@trafford.com

10 9 8 7 6 5 4 3 2 1

This book is dedicated to all of my clients, colleagues, family and friends that have, over the years, allowed me to share with them my passion for how beautiful this country of Costa Rica truly is, as well as my parents who inspired me and showed me the way, and, of course, my wonderful wife and girls, who are making this journey in paradise a unique and loving experience.

TABLE OF CONTENTS

DISCLAIMER

We've made our best effort to give you the most accurate assessment of the real estate market here in Costa Rica, given our years of experience from coast to golden coast. Every attempt has been made to ensure that the information provided in these pages is up-to-date and relevant to meet your needs.

But, please keep in mind that this is Costa Rica, a country of rapid change and fast-paced growth, with very different circumstances than those you might be familiar with in North America and Europe. And, as they do everywhere else in the world—laws are amended. Also, we'd like to acknowledge that while we've made every effort to be accurate in all research, background work, and advice, there is always the possibility for error on our part.

With the learned guidance offered in this book, even before selecting a competent, skilled real estate professional, you should feel confident that with the information provided you will be able to purchase or sell real estate in Costa Rica. But, even if you do not face a complicated situation—which could come out of nowhere in this country of beauty and pura vida-we recommend you consult a real estate agent who is affiliated with one of the two local real estate associations so that you may have the best professional assistance in navigating the legal real estate situation in Costa Rica, while confident you are covered by the best ethical guidelines in the world.

PROFESSIONALISM AND SECURITY IN A NATION LACKING REAL ESTATE LAWS

by Orlando Lopez,
CEO of Stewart Title Latin America
(Title insurance company)

In Costa Rica, anybody can legally sell you real estate, no licensing is required. There's no guarantee that what you see, what you pay for, is what you are going to get in the end. Fortunately, since 1997, Stewart Title has operated in Costa Rica, shutting down the risk in the market for buyers and investors with our commitment to relationships with those individuals and companies who operate according to the highest standards, in compliance with the realtor legal framework and ethical practices. Nicholas Viale, at the helm of his CENTURY 21 Coastal Estates Group, has certainly been one of those individuals. With an international education, a deep love for Costa Rica, in particular, and extensive history in real estate, he has instilled at his firm a fervor to provide their clients with the most comprehensive investment knowledge possible in the business. Every agent is constantly upgrading their education on every possible aspect of real estate. Not a day goes by that the company's broad range of services, and Costa Rican-wide reach is not explored, providing clients with personalized, factual information that ends in profitable results for all.

Certainly, we are proud of the business relationship and friendship that we at Stewart Title have developed over the years with Nicholas and his firm. We are equally inspired by the hope of a consolidated real estate market in Costa Rica, one that is professional and safe for investors to thrive.

ABOUT THE AUTHOR

Nicholas Viale explains that real estate was always in his blood: While a young man on the French Rivera, his father was developing real estate projects and his mother was-and still is-a luxury real estate broker. So, Viale knew to begin his own real estate career right here in his home country. For over 12 years he sold and helped developing big projects in the South of France, before moving to Costa Rica in 1995 , where he fell in love with Tamarindo's stunning natural beauty.

That year, Viale decided to open a branch of his company in Costa Rica, with his first real estate office in Tamarindo, as well as developing his initial condo project in the blossoming tropical beach town, the vacation villas called *Pueblo del Mar.*

By 1996, he had moved all his operations to Costa Rica, and three years later, made the critical decision to enjoin his office with CENTURY 21 Costa Rica. Since that time, his company CENTURY 21 Coastal Estates-whose headquarters are based on Tamarindo's main boulevard but now boasts several offices along Costa Rica's Pacific coast-has been one of the top producing franchises for his newly adopted country of Costa Rica, as well as the Central American region.

As owner of CENTURY 21 Coastal Estates, Viale utilizes his knowledge and degree in Business Management from the University of Nice-France as a jump-off point for continual study of the laws, policies and procedures that make up the smartest real estate deals He and his staff institute, attend and address nationa and international seminars on the evolving financia and legal markets pertaining to construction and development in order to provide the best services to their clients.

Viale himself has served as President of the Costa Rica Global Association of Realtors (CRGAR) from 2004 -05 . One of his highest achievements during that time was the signing of a partnership in 2004 between the United States-based National Association of Realtors® (NAR) and the International Consortium of Real Estate Associations (ICREA) in order to agree on a common code of ethics, one that would develop and promote a global multi-listing-system (MLS) that would raise the standards of the real estate industry.

Today, CENTURY 21 Coastal Estates is the largest and most trusted real estate network in the country, serving the best beach areas such as: Playa Tamarindo, Playa Langosta, Playa Grande, Playa Avellanas, Playa Conchal, Flamingo, Jaco, Herradura, and other secret spots. Nicholas is still a member of CRGAR® and of NAR®, as is his staff.

His business philosophy centers around three ironclad tenets: knowledge, honesty, and integrity. Viale believes these characteristics are not only the key to a successful and profitable career, but also to a mutually beneficial long-standing business relationship with his clients. His company, CENTURY 21 Coastal Estates, is specialized in the second homes market-including houses, condominiums, gated communities-putting into practice his years of Costa Rican real estate experience the understanding that when investing in this tropical paradise, high-end buyers desire homes that blend the finest amenities with comfort and a casual lifestyle.

Viale's commitment to community has been a priority since he immersed himself into the Costa Rican lifestyle all those years ago. He was the Vice President of Tamarindo's Chamber of Commerce from 2002-2003, before becoming board member of Tamarindo's Pro Mejoras in 2003-2004 , an organization of townspeople formed to make the area better by improving the roads, security, parks, and more.

His company will often participate in local fundraisers. As a matter of fact, in 2006, CENTURY 21 Coast al Estates itself organized an open international charity surf tournament to benefit the local beach environmental groups including the Blue Flag Committee, the Surfrider Foundation, and the Tamarindo Lifeguards.

CENTURY 21 Coastal Estates also participated in a fundraiser in Miami, Florida to benefit Easter Seals, the non-profit, community-based health agency dedicated to helping children and adults with disabilities.

When not working and running CENTURY 21 Coastal Estates, or taking care of his local responsibilities, Nicholas can be found with his wife and two daughters, either at home in nearby Playa Langosta, or on that town's beautiful beach at sunset. His family, which includes their dog *Foster*, loves the ocean.

"I love my life here," Viale says. "Costa Ricans are very friendly and educated people, and the nature is wonderful. It's a really fun and exciting experience for me, my family and my business partners to be part of this growing community of Tamarindo. We have the best quality of life with nice sunsets, good waves and tropical days and nights."

A PASSION FOR REAL ESTATE

A PASSION FOR REAL ESTATE

I have been in real estate all my life.

My father was a successful real estate developer, nd my mother a top luxury real estate broker. Let ne tell you that at home, we had just one subject of onversation. I had breakfast, lunch and dinner with eal estate. And, when I had some spare time, I would ass it with my father on construction sites-my pleasant nemories of climbing on the backhoe or the crane ith him remain in my head. Or I would go to my mother's office as the Telex clanked incessantly well before the first computer, fax machine or manageable cell phone.

For me, it was natural to move into that world after earning my college degree. By this time, it was the mid-'80s, and the real estate market was booming in the south of France, so sales agents were in high demand.

That's how I ended up spending my days and weekends in sales offices working for developers in charge of the pre-sales of their inventory. After a few semesters, my name became known on the market and I could choose from the many projects which ones I wanted to work for. My career in real estate had just begun...

Needless to say, I had-and have-a real passion for real estate, and a deep respect for my clients, keeping in mind how important the process of buying or selling property is for them, whether the transaction is their first residential home, one of many vacation properties or even a simple investment.

There is no day that I have to go to the office that I am not happy. I generally get there early and am one of the last to leave. My father would say that when you really like what you are doing, 24 hours a day are not enough to do all you would like to do, and that's exactly how I feel about my work. I just love it.

To me, because there is nothing more important than investing in real estate, I decided to write this book and pass along what have become my family values. These were ideals I learned from both my father and mother.

Let's start with THREE simple lessons:

1. Real estate is a SIGNIFICANT PURCHASE. We are talking about a lot of money here. It's not like buying a new flat screen TV or a new computer, it's about spending a lot more, sometimes involving a mortgage that is going to have an direct effect on your life and your family's financial structure. And, you don't want to mess with that, especially, if you have a family and kids and want to secure your future or if you want to retire and keep the lifestyle in which you are accustomed.

2. The STRATEGY involved in your purchase is very important. Whether you need a roof over your family's head, a vacation retreat, extra rental income, or a long-term investment, the strategy will all be the same. You are building a real estate portfolio, one that will help you save money and create wealth for you and your family. This is an important move in today's economy and that decision deserves all your attention.

3. This investment WILL CHANGE YOUR LIFE Let's stop for a minute and have a look at your future Do you think that in the next years the cost of education for your kids will go down? Do you think the gas prices will go down? What about the price of a meal at your favorite restaurant or the cost of a retirement home? don't think so either. This is called inflation...and you can be sure about one thing: All your living costs are going to increase significantly in the next few years. This will occur more than you think and for many reasons, such as the demographic boom, lack of basic resources and materials such as gas, steel, and even gold-all of our living costs are going to rise. It's been anticipated and predicted by several famous gurus, and we should pay attention to that. The good news is that there is a solution in order to maintain your current lifestyle, or simply in order to prepare for your future: You need to build equity right now, right away.

One of the safest and best ways to build wealth and to secure your future is to invest in real estate. Sure, you have heard this song already, but honestly, how many of you that have listened to this tune actually own your main residence? Are you already generating extra income from ownership of a rental property? How many of you have secured your future needs and your kids' education by starting investing and creating a private real estate investment trust?

If you answered, 'no' to any of those questions, now is the time to heed the call to action.

Since I came to Costa Rica and started real estate operations, I have continued the family legacy, and doing what I, myself, have been doing all my life: selling real estate and passionately helping clients. It's not always been easy, but I've been smart. You should be too. Did you know that in Costa Rica real estate licensing is not required to buy and sell property? Did you know, that in case anything goes wrong, it could take months, and in some cases YEARS to file a civil lawsuit in Costa Rica?

I bet you didn't.

That being said, I don't want you to trust ANY real estate company or any so-called, self-designed real estate agent in order to handle your important investment decisions.

That indeed is another purpose for my writing this book, to give you, in as simple a manner as possible global knowledge of the local real estate market as well as some useful tips and facts that will help you plan your investment strategy.

Let me finish my personal section with these words, pronounced in 2005 at the National Association of Realtors® (NAR) international convention in San Francisco during my introductory speech as President of the Costa Rican Global Association of Realtors (CRGAR). At that time, we were signing a historical partnership between both of these associations:

"Times are changing, people are working less, traveling more, exploring new countries and continents, and it is sometimes tempting to invest in real estate while you are on vacation...

It's tempting...

...as long as you get a good understanding of the local real estate laws and regulations,

...as long as you don't waste your precious time visiting random properties in a unknown country,

...and as long as your investment is processed and registered by qualified real estate professionals.

And that is exactly what our partnership is all about: Giving our clients the right tools and connections in order to make the process of buying and selling real estate, Easier, Faster, and Secure.

This book is also a partnership between myself and you, and I sincerely hope you will get as much pleasure reading it, as I had writing it. Investing in real estate in Costa Rica can be a very rewarding experience if it's done the right way and with the right help and assistance.

In the end, it's all about sharing a common passion: a passion for real estate, as well as a passion for our little tropical paradise...

IN FEW WORDS...

Investing in real estate is the best and safest way to build wealth and secure your future, and what works if you invest in your hometown also works if you invest in a foreign country. Investing in real estate is a very important statement and life-changing event. That is the reason why you should—just as any other important event in your life—surround yourself with the best partners, the best pros in the market, people with passion and deep respect for their work. Their passion will be the life insurance of your investment, your future and your retirement.

CONSTITUTION OF
THE REPUBLIC OF COSTA RICA

ARTICLE 19. Foreigers have the same individual and social rights and duties that Costa Ricans do, with the exceptions and limitations established by this Constitution and the laws.

They may not intervene in the political affairs of the country, being subject to the jurisdiction of the courts of justice and the authorities of the Republic, and may not resort to diplomatic channels, except as provided in international conventions.

PART ONE

A PLACE CALLED COSTA RICA

A PLACE CALLED COSTA RICA

Over the years, I have seen a lot of visitors in Costa Rica on vacation. Most of them already knew the best beaches, tours and local restaurants, but only few were aware of this country's rich history and glorious past.

The thing is, as I said, most people come to Costa Rica on vacations, and at that time are not planning on investing in real estate. So why bother with the history and facts of a country, right? After few cocktails, awe-inspiring sunsets with serenades on the beach (not necessarily in that order), they fall in love with the country, and it's not long before they understand the various benefits of investing in this little corner of paradise....

Investors soon grow to learn that the history of Costa Rica is as rich as the country itself and is a reason why its people are so genuine and so friendly.

I want to help you with that process. What follows are some historic and cultural facts that you will find useful about this wonderful nation that you might one day call Home.

Although Costa Rica received its name from Gil Gonzalez Davila, a member of Spanish explorer Christopher Columbus's 1502 crew; archaeologists date the country's existence back 10,000 years prior citing pre-Columbian mysteries such as the perfect granite spheres-called bolas-that remain today around the west coast and range in size from baseballs to large cars. In addition, the recent discovery of Guayabo an ancient city with aqueducts dating to 1.000 B.C located 30 miles east of San Jose-and littered with gold and jade-further substantiate those claims, as do archeological sites in the central highlands and Nicoya peninsula which show the influence from the Mexican Olmec and Nahuatl civilizations.

By the time Columbus arrived near Limón, there were four major indigenous tribes living in Costa Rica: the east's Caribs, while the Borucas, Chibchas, and Diquis resided in the southwest. The explorer noticed the Caribs wearing gold, returned to Europe to tell of it, but the adventurers who followed found the natives hostile and European colonization in Costa Rican failed for 50 years, moving north and south instead.

Toiling away under Spanish rule via Guatemala with Cartago, Costa Rica as its capital from 1562 until the late 18th Century, the Costa Ricans eventually improved its economic conditions with exports of wheat and tobacco before gaining independence from Spain on September 15, 1821. Yet, the country remained in conflict, torn by the choice to join the newly independent Mexico or a new group of Central American states. Inside Costa Rica, battle lines were drawn between

San Jose and Alajuela leaders and their counterparts in pro-Mexican Cartago and Heredia. Then, in 1823, civil war ensued, albeit briefly, before Costa Rica finally joined the Central American confederation.

Costa Rica's first head of state was Juan Mora Fernandez, who was elected by the people in 1824. His best claim to fame was land reforms, and he followed a progressive course, but inadvertently created an elite class of powerful coffee barons, who eventually overthrew the nation's first president, Jose Maria Castro, who was succeeded by Juan Rafael Mora.

Under Mora's leadership, Costa Rica fought back the infamous North American William Walker, a disgruntled southerner who thought that the United States should annex Central America and turn it into a slave state. A noted lunatic, and very dangerous, he put together an army of about 50 men, just after he had invaded Mexico-where he had been captured and then released back to the States-then set forth into Panama where he briefly seized control before being forced to flee-into Costa Rica. After his bid for tyrannical rule in his country, he was defeated by Mora's forces!

Walker then focused on Honduras, who captured him, and finally, the man was executed.

Political turmoil remained the norm within Costa Rica for the next decade or so. General Tomas Guardia seized power in 1870, ruling as a military dictator for 2 years and marking progressive policies like free and compulsory primary education, and reeling in the excesses of the military and taxing coffee earnings to finance public works. He also initiated the construction of the Atlantic railroad from San Jose to the Caribbean by Minor Keith.

The first free elections took place in 1889, and Costa Rica moved into full democracy.

After the election of Dr. Rafael Angel Calderon Guardia in 1940, he implemented an enlightened land reform, a guaranteed minimum wage and progressive taxation, but his United Social Christian Party refused to step down after losing the 1948 election, and another civil war took place. Opposed by José Maria Figueres Ferrer, and supported by the governments of

Guatemala and Cuba, he won this 40-day war.

Costa Rica's positive change continued under Figueres, who became head of the Founding Junta of the Second Republic of Costa Rica. He banned the Communist Party, gave women the right to vote granted full citizenship to blacks, established a term limit for presidents, and nationalized the banks and insurance companies. In probably the most significant move in the country and arguable the most notable peace mark in the world, Figueres abolished the army of Costa Rica in 1948.

He also founded the Partido de Liberacion Nacional (PLN won the 2006 presidential election with current Costa Rica President, Nobel Peace Prize Winner Oscar Arias. As a matter of fact, during Arias' first term a president in the late 1980s, he earned that Nobel Peace Prize while Nicaragua was embroiled in a civil war, and he got the five Central American presidents to sign his peace plan in 1987 in Guatemala City.) When Figueres died in 1990, Costa Rica remained a peaceful stable country in Central America, a politically unstable region.

Today, Costa Rica draws people from around the globe, making tourism one of the country's main sources of income. One of its primary lures is the fact that it's a democratic and peaceful country, without an army. It's other attraction is that with only .03% and surface on the planet, this nation holds 6% of the existing biodiversity in the entire world, at the same time that 25.58% of the country is conserved and naturally protected territory.

Costa Rica's richness also lies with the cultural diversity of its populace, made up of the indigenous Bribri, Cabecar, Maleku, Teribe, Boruca, Ngöbe, Huetar, and Chorotega, as well as the immigrants who settled here after Columbus' time including those of European ancestry, as well as Africans, Asians, Middle Eastern, Israeli and those from different places on the North American continent. The *Ticos*, as Costa Ricans are commonly known, are famous for their hospitality, high education level, hard-work ethic, and extremely friendly disposition. It's not uncommon to hear that Ticos are this country's greatest asset!

Even with a 1% indigenous population, their lifestyle is everywhere-from a typical Costa Rica meal to the handmade artifacts and souvenirs to the fiestas featuring bull rides all over the provinces. The Spanish language and its architecture cull from European influence.

Geographically, Costa Rica is made up of rocky highlands, which run throughout most of the country and range from approximately 1,000 to 2,000 meters (3,000 to 6,000 feet above sea level). The Guanacaste Mountain Range, Central Mountain Range, and Talamanca Mountain Range are the main ranges extending the entire length of the nation. There are several active volcanoes (Arenal Volcano, Irazu Volcano, Rincon de la Vieja Volcano and Turrialba Volcano) and the country's highest mountain is Chirripo Hill with a height of 3,819 m/12,530 feet. Costa Rica has a relatively long coastline on both the Atlantic and Pacific Ocean sides-with world renowned surf break and fishing spots-as well as a number of rivers and streams that attract specialist kayakers and rafters from all over the world.

The beautiful climate, with natural breezes cooling down the coasts and mild mountain temperatures, is one facet that attracts tourists to Costa Rica. The average annual temperatures range from 31.7°C (89°F) on the coast to 16.7°C (62°F) inland. Dry Season-occurs December through April, with Green Season-also as Rainy Season-running May to December. However, don't be worried about that term Rainy Season; it could rain a little bit, or a lot, depending on your location in the country and the time of month.

Unique to Costa Rica is the quality and affordability of its healthcare. As a matter of fact, non-residents will find low-cost, excellent medical services, personnel, facilities and hospitals, while Ticos and residents receive top-level pension and social security via Costa Rica's Social Security Service (CCSS). This is partially why the country has the highest life expectancy rate in Latin America at 77.75 years old. Child care is equally superb, with one of the lowest infant mortality rates in the world at 10.82%.

Without a military, money is invested in public education. In Costa Rica, there are nearly 6,147 elementary, middle, and high schools and more than 50 universities in the country, with bilingual and international public and private elementary, secondary schools for children of all nationalities with a variety of curriculums to satisfy any particular needs.

Banks, both state-owned and privately held, are everywhere. The *colon (or colones)* is the official currency; however, US dollars are widely accepted. US dollars and traveler's checks can be changed in banks and hotels. Most major credit cards are widely accepted, and cash advances can be obtained at banks around the country. ATM machines are popular now not only in San Jose but in most beach towns and tourist centers.

It's pretty clear when you are in the mountain ranges looking at the coffee, cow pastures, bananas, and other crops, that agriculture is a huge contributor to Costa Rica's economy. Historically, coffee had been the country's most important crop, and to this day continue to be some of the best in the world. Just check out the airport when the tourists are leaving and see how much gets purchased on the way out of the country!

Yet in this day and age, the *double Ts*, are taking over the economic coffers of Costa Rica. That would be *tourism* and *technology*. According to reports, visitors and their dollars are earning more than any one exported crop during the last few years, and projections only look more favorable. Of course, microchips and the internet are a wide open Latin economic playing field.

With all of this factual information at your fingertips, you now have a better understanding of Costa Rica, its history, culture and industry. Now, you've got a taste of Pura Vida living!

For more information about Costa Rica you can visit the official website from the Instituto Costaricense de Turismo www.visitcostarica.com (National Tourism Institute).

IN FEW WORDS...

Costa Rica is the oldest democracy in Central America.

The government is very stable, the economy balanced between tourism, and agriculture, and the level of education is definitively unparalleled when compared to the neighboring countries.

Its natural beauty, incredible flora and fauna, active volcanoes, unspoiled beaches and friendly people, contribute to make Costa Rica the #1 vacation destination in Central America...a tropical paradise located only few hours away from your home.

PART TWO

WELCOME TO
PARADISE!

WELCOME TO PARADISE

"Welcome to Paradise!"

That's how we greet our clients when they arrive in he country for the very first time, before this tropical 1aven becomes their second home.

After all these years spent in Costa Rica, I've seen 1 lot of first-time visitors who, as I did back all those 'ears ago-fall in love with this beautiful nation, with its)reathtaking sunsets, its welcoming and friendly people, unspoiled sand beaches, incredible natural mountains and trees, and free wildlife, then make a decision to change their lives. They want an exclusive place here in this part of Central America, a tropical retreat to call their own.

Over the years, Costa Rica has had an incredible tourism boom, and with it has come an even bigger increase in the amount of vacationers who turn around and invest in a future here as well. Overall, national tourism has risen an average of 4.9% annually, with 1.7 million visitors in 2006, generating profits cited by the World Organization of Tourism as around $1.6 million. The Costa Rican Institute of Tourism (ICT) reports growth near 6.6% with an expected 2.3 million tourists entering the country annually by 2012. That's good news for you; it means as tourism continues to skyrocket, so will the real estate possibilities!

Nowadays, there's no need to just take my word for it. Reputable international media organizations back this up as well. This year, CNBC reported Costa Rica as "the hottest real estate market on the planet," while an article published April 2007 in the *Latin Business*

Chronicle predicted that: "Despite a rise in real estate prices and an explosion in hotel rooms, Costa Rica's real estate market-already one of the fastest-growing in Latin America-has a bright outlook, experts say." Foreign investment in Costa Rican real estate amounted to $177 million in 2004, $225 million in 2005, and is expected to reach $850 million by 2011, which is a sign of a booming industry.

The famed *New York Times*, in a Real Estate section cover story explained just some of the reasons for the investment frenzy: "Costa Rica has the advantages of an active tourism board and a reputation as peaceful and environmentally friendly. It also has the longest tradition of democracy in Latin America."

Baby-boomers love Costa Rica: It's the proximity to the United States, its tropical climate, the Latino lifestyle, the extremely low living and healthcare costs, plus the affordable real estate prices-especially when compared to traditional US vacation destinations such as California, Florida and Hawaii. As a matter of fact, the US government predicts that over the next 10 years, more than 1 million baby-boomers will retire in Costa Rica.

Finally, by the time I was nearing completion of this book in 2007, I noticed that Costa Rica had, for the second time in a row, won the award of the Best Destination in Latin America from *Travel Weekly* magazine. That award is a result of votes cast by more than 120,000 magazine readers (source: *The Guanacaste Journal*), all members of the US tourism industry who considered that Costa Rica is a quality tourism spot, and maintains good services and countless attractions. Interesting to note as well that by winning these awards, Costa Rica was defeating countries such as Panama, Nicaragua, Chile, Peru, Argentina and Brazil.

Some of our clients over the past years understood the opportunities of investing in our little piece of paradise, and with the time and experience, anticipated market moves, such as tourism growth.

Sound tempting to you, too?

That is exactly what this book is all about: I want to

give you the education, tools and connections in order to make the process of buying and selling real estate in Costa Rica ...

... Easier, Faster, and Secure.

So let's get started.

IN FEW WORDS...

Tourism in Costa Rica is booming, attracting major companies, international hotel brands and industries, as well as the expected attendant real estate investments. This has been a real shot in the arm for the local economy and guarantees the country's future.

Recently, Costa Rica has recently been ranked Best Destination in Latin America by *Travel Weekly* magazine, defeating its neighbors and friends Panama, Nicaragua, Chile, Peru, Argentina and Brazil.

Tourism is booming in paradise... and it's just the beginning!

PART THREE

WHY YOU SHOULD INVEST IN COSTA RICA NOW

WHY YOU SHOULD INVEST
IN COSTA RICA NOW

This is exactly what I wanted to know when I first visited Costa Rica in 1995. Why and how? What would be my goals and my strategy? And, why now?

In this chapter, I will give you 12 good reasons to invest in Costa Rica. Believe me, there are many more than 12 to offer, but I guess I just like that number.

Before we get there, I would like to tell you how you should invest. By this I mean, what should be your strategy and guidelines. During all these years selling vacation homes in famous resort destinations (first in the south of France, followed, of course, here in Costa Rica), I have seen a variety of buyers; each one had a different dream and a different strategy and I have seen which ones worked and which did not. I have learned how to avoid some very common mistakes. It's now the time and the place to share that with you.

Generally, in the vacation homes market, you will find two kinds of investors. The first one is what we call the "classic" investor: very conservative and well aware of the benefits of putting his money in a hot vacation destination's real estate market. That investor will analyze the market components and structure before making his offer. But, an interesting fact about that financier is his long-term strategy. His plan will indicate that he keep his investment for a minimum period of three to five years before eventually re-selling it. Why is that? Well, because that allows for the generation of a net 8-12% rental income-which is common in a renowned destination-and at the same time get the benefits of a 15-25% increase in value per year. And I have to add, that in booming times or new markets, I have seen higher rates.

At the opposite end of the spectrum is the *speculator-flipper*. We give them this name because they put a property under contract then immediately put it back on the market for sale-flip it-in order to make some quick profits. Their strategy is completely different: Time is of the essence and they don't wait to create added value on their investment (for example by generating rental income). They generally are outnumbered when the market is booming. In short, they come with about 5-10% down for a deposit, and try to resell the property immediately. If they are lucky, they net the same amount they deposited; if they are unfortunate, or if the timing of their investment is not appropriate, hey loose it all.

If you are a flipper, you have just bought yourself he wrong book. This book will not teach you how to become millionaire in few weeks-as I heard in some nvestment seminars I attended recently. This book will not teach you how to retire tomorrow and live well from buying and flipping properties-another *memorable* real estate class I attended.

What you will learn from this book is how to have a cohesive and consistent approach to your investment in paradise. And, guess what? You might end-up a millionaire and retire rich one day as have many of our clients. But you have to be patient and well-informed first.

There is nothing that disturbs me more than flippers. I'm sure you've been able to detect that in my writing, right? They don't bring anything to our industry-especially no cash inflow-and they generate an increase in demand, which ends up creating a false boost in offers and prices. In other words, flippers produce all the ingredients for what we call the *rea estate bubble*. The real estate bubble consists in a virtua boom of the industry that will most of the time end up in a market-crash due to the lack of appropriate inventory and qualified buyers, followed by an adjustment period, in the best of the cases, or a major crisis of real estate, in other cases.

This is exactly the situation that happened in the US and Europe during the 1990s, causing an unprecedented crisis, the largest and longest one since World War II.

This situation also happened most recently during the 2001-2005 real estate boom and ended up in 2006 in a crisis marked by the desappearance of the speculators-flippers, leaving the market to serious buyers.

With all that being said, investing in a foreign country-particularly Costa Rica-is always a sensible experience. Even if you are a classic investor, your knowledge will be useful up to a certain point. Then you will have to deal with unfamiliar laws and regulations, other practices and contract forms, and additional market mechanics.

However, when faced with facts and figures from various news reports and Costa Rican tourism statistics, you're still not convinced that you should make this most sound financial decision to invest in tropical paradise.

I understand completely, which is why you're

looking to a licensed, qualified real estate professional with an understanding of the local real estate laws and regulations to consult you in these matters.

To that end, let me give you 12 good reasons why it's essential that you invest right now in Costa Rica:

1. BECAUSE YOU CAN:

Right to invest and own real estate is open to everyone.

As a foreigner you are legally permitted to invest and own real estate in Costa Rica. This is generally the first information our clients want to know when they start the investigation process. The most comprehensive form of property ownership in Costa Rica is *fee simple ownership*. The concept of fee simple ownership is the same in Costa Rica as in the US. Basically, foreigners have the same rights as Costa Rican people, and that includes the right to purchase and own real estate in their name or through a corporation, the right to use it and to enjoy it without restrictions, and also the right to get rental income from your investment and to resell it whenever you want. You don't need native partners or any local trust (as in other countries such as Mexico); neither citizenship nor residency or even a presence in the country is required for private ownership.

2. CONSTITUTIONAL OWNERSHIP ENTITLEMENT

Private property in Costa Rica is unchallengeable and guaranteed by the Constitution. There is no restriction to ownership of real estate in Costa Rica with the exception of direct beachfront property in particular cases called concession land. And even in that case, one can still own concession property, with a few applied restrictions that any corporate or real estate lawyer can help you fully understand. Further, some beachfront properties in various specific areas-especially on the North and Central Pacific coasts-are fully titled and therefore can be entirely owned by foreigners without any restrictions.

To own the remaining Costa Rican territory is a rock-solid right as allowed and protected by the Constitution.

3. THE BOOM OF TOURISM INDUSTRY

Costa Rica is still a growing tourist destination which will only increase the value of property. In 2006, the US Central Intelligence Agency World Fact Book ranked Costa Rica as one of five countries that stands "head and shoulders above all other nations worldwide in terms of the potential their real estate markets present property investors" while affirming that the government has successfully established an "economically and politically stable country in which more overseas investors are focusing their financial interests."

That's why construction grew by 64%, particularly in the North-Pacific beach areas. "Prices still remain lower than they are in more developed countries, and that's driving the continuing growth in construction," said Jaime Molina, President of the Costa Rican Construction Chamber.

Investing in Costa Rica right now is the smartest financial decision you can make at this moment, especially if you take into consideration the potential increased value of property in this country. The current influx of multimillion dollar investments-ranging from international hotel chains such as Four Seasons, J.W. Marriott, Hilton, Mandarin-Occidental, Ritz-Carlton, the Canyon Ranch and Spa group, Hyatt, Regent International, Westin Hotels, Aman Resorts, Rosewood Hotels, and St. Regis, to PepsiCo's big influx of cash in Guanacaste to Steve Case's (AOL founder) ventures and many more across the nation-will be bringing a number of high-end luxury developments in the next one to five years. Up to a dozen golf courses are either in place or on the drawing board as well. With this, property premiums for everyone are expected go sky high.

4. THE NATURAL BEAUTY AND CULTURE

Concurrently, Costa Rica is a true eco-paradise with a friendly Latino people!

The Costa Rican idea-Pura Vida or Pure Life-is engrained in the culture of the country's gracious, educated, helpful, unhurried, and environmentally aware people. Which bodes well, since for such a tiny nation, Costa Rica has plenty of natural treasures to behold—5% of the world's biodiversity in the form of plants and animals. The government actually protects over 25% of its national territory within its National Park System or National Wildlife Refuges, Biological Reserves, Protection Zones and Absolute Nature Reserves. While those areas make up a quarter of Costa Rican territory, there are still enough beautiful coastlines to surf, fish, scuba, sail and snorkle. And there are rivers and lakes to explore. The 13 live volcanoes provide majestic light shows, not to mention support ecosystems of cloud, and rainforests. Lower down, in the dry forests, there too exist a plethoria of flora and fauna to admire.

According to *Future Brand*, an internationally prestigious data analysis assessment company, Costa Rica continues to be an attractive natural paradise for tourists and is a "Rising Star" among the ten most acclaimed countries ranked with the most probability and opportunities of growth in the next five years. In its published findings, Future Brand also ranked the country among the top ten countries in the world for its natural beauty and its unique culture.

5. CLOSE PROXIMITY TO NORTH AMERICA

Two international airports set those beautiful beaches only a few hours away from your own doorstep. San Jose's Juan Santamaria Airport is just a Nature Air or Sansa flight away from Guanacaste's Gold Coast, or a simple one-hour-and-a-half drive to the Central Pacific beaches where colorful macaws make their daily aerial circles!

Cámara de Turismo Guanacasteca (CATURGUA)

predict passenger movement at Liberia's Daniel Oduber International at 400,000 for 2007, and expect as many as 1 million to use that new $20 million passenger terminal at the airport by 2017. And Liberia's facility is very close to that province's beaches. I remember once I took a 7:00 a.m. flight back from Boston where I was visiting a client. By noon, I was having lunch at a beachfront restaurant with my family in Tamarindo.

6. SAFE AND SECURE COUNTRY

Costa Rica is one of the safest places to live on the planet. Think about this: With the insecurity the world is facing now with terrorism and war, Costa Rica became the first country ever to constitutionally abolish its army in 1948. Costa Rican people love peace, and the nation is an exception in Latin America, where military dictatorships have long dominated politics. Costa Rica has had more than 100 years of democratic tradition and it has the most stable government in the Central American region.

As a matter of fact, the current President Oscar Arias, received the 1987 Nobel Peace Prize. After becoming Costa Rican President the first time in 1986, he became critically involved against the activities of US-backed *Contras* in his country's territory. Arias focused on drawing Nicaragua-where the focus of the Contra-Sandanista conflict was based-as well as the other Central American countries, into an peace mission for the entire region. In May of that year, he met with the Presidents of Guatemala, El Salvador, Honduras, and Nicaragua to discuss his own peace plan. In early 1987, at a new gathering a revised accord was approved by the five presidents in Guatemala. History was made, and the isthmus remains stable today.

7. REASONABLY PRICED INVESTMENTS

Real Estate prices are very affordable when compared to the United States and other international second homes' markets. Remember that as a foreigner here, you are, by law as written in the Constitution, allowed to invest and own real estate in Costa Rica.

Well, the good news is that PARADISE IS STILL AFFORDABLE! No matter how high a price you plan on paying with your first investment in Costa Rica, you will find they are competitive, especially when going for it in the pre-construction stage.

For example, let's say you decide to get your feet wet purchasing a seaside or ocean view vacation condo that you will use for yourself, your family and friends, and then use it to generate rental income the rest of the year. How much do you think it will cost you for a 700 square-feet, one-bedroom unit? Well, you can get that for under 120K!

Need a larger unit? Two bedroom units are priced from 150K and three-bedrooms fall under 180K. We are talking about condos with excellent features such as anti-seismic construction, traditional building techniques and quality materials, kitchen furnished with granite counter-tops and air conditioning throughout However, if you are looking for a dream house located beachfront or overlooking the bay and its breathtaking sunsets, the local market also offers a wide variety of luxury homes and condos priced from the 250s, way below US prices.

8. VIRTUALLY NO REAL ESTATE TAXES

Costa Rica is a tax-friendly destination when it comes to real estate investments. More succinctly, the country has extremely low property taxes, and no tax on capital gains or inheritances. That's really GOOD NEWS!

Let's just touch on a few numbers: Property Tax, how much do you think that you will be paying each year? Merely .25% in property tax. Which means, if your condo is valuated at $100K you will pay $250 annually in property tax. This tax is actually the only existing tax applicable to real estate at the moment.

As to capital gains taxes in Costa Rica? 0%, Nada, Niente, Nothing, there are no capital gain taxes in Costa Rica (unless you are a developer). That means clearly the profit you make on each resale can be fully re-invested, allowing you to build a solid portfolio legally and in record time. It's not surprising that some of our clients living in the US, Canada or even Europe liquidated their investments in their respective countries and reinvested most of that cash-or even all of it-in Costa Rica.

And, finally, inheritance taxes? Same thing, 0% which means the capital you've worked to earn your entire life will be fully transferred to your family, a detail I think is very important.

Of course, some might worry that property tax will increase in the future. And it may, considering the actual rate or the declared values of the property is in some cases way below the real value to begin with. However, you can bet that this will generate more local infrastructure investments from the authorities, which will have very positive results on your investment.

9. FIRST-CLASS PERSONNEL AND RESOURCES

High-quality construction materials used at the beaches, in the mountains, in the jungles, in the forests

Exotic woods grown in the forests of Guanacaste are often found in homes constructed by eminent developers, while the highest quality, most modern brands and finishing are used in homes, condos and properties at even the most difficult, exclusive destinations.

10. ESTABLISHED LAND REGISTRY

Costa Rica offers one of the best, safest and controlled legal systems including a national land registry, title insurance and escrow services available throughout the country. The Registro Nacional is an established land registry, and all information regarding every property in Costa Rica is filled, registered and available to all of this country's real estate professionals. In our offices for example, all of our computers are linked to the Registro Nacional, and we can immediately get the status on any property and follow through to inform our clients about it. And if that is not sufficient, keep in mind that most of the major, US-based, title insurance companies are represented in Costa Rica, among them Stewart Title, which has been operating in the country since 1997, offering full services of title insurance, escrow, closings, and most recently, local financing.

11. FINANCING FOR FOREIGNERS

Local financing is readily available for foreigners investing in Costa Rica. As non-residential foreigners who want to purchase land, condos or houses, you now have the option of real estate loans from Costa Rican national and private banks which give comparable conditions to United States banks. Our company is currently working with some of the best mortgage brokers and banks in the country offering special conditions for foreigners investing in Costa Rica (in some specific cases up to 85% financing over 25 years amortization period). We are also connected with some of the top mortgage companies in the U.S. offering the latest in second home mortgage and refinancing, and we generally help our clients to find a custom-designed solution to their financing needs in record time.

But that's not all; did you know that you can buy real estate in Costa Rica using your IRA (Individual

Retirement Account)? Perhaps you don't realize that while your IRA has been your personal savings plan providing income tax advantages for retirement purposes, it is also legally usable for investment in real estate-even in a foreign country! (This is true with other retirement funds as well.) I have witnessed several of my clients over the past years legally using their IRA to purchase residential or commercial real estate in our tropical paradise. You might want to check into that option as well. To do so, look for more information and FAQ about IRAs, at www.IRA.com

12. EARN MONEY TOO!

Your new Costa Rican home or condo is a tremendous income producing source. The latest trend among the savvy tourist is to forgo the typical lodging option of a hotel, instead renting a fully equipped luxury condominium, villa or house, according to *Travel & Leisure Magazine*. This is fantastic for you, particularly if you have just purchased a Costa Rican home or condo with a kitchen and multiple bedrooms that are extremely comfortable, with on-site services that make everything easy for a holiday.

Condominiums offer more amenities than a hotel, more flexibility for a person and their family, such as the opportunity to prepare or obtain breakfast at anytime-day or night. The units afford more privacy for one's group, no matter how big or small. In most cases, renting a condo or apartment for a traveler is going to be less expensive than a hotel room, especially if the tourist is in a large party and shares expenses with other family members and friends. This is why we've been observing a real increase in short-term condo rentals lately, especially in the leasing of those units with 2- to 3-bedrooms.

Imagine that you own a city home and you rent it long term, you can expect a 3-6% net return per year. Well, if you have a vacation home or condo that you rent on short term basis (maximum for 1 week), you can expect a minimum net return of 8% and a maximum 12-15% per year. But, that's not all. Let's talk abou the added value. We all know that real estate in resort destination is more dynamic than in other areas. Why is that? Not only are you renting an apartment, but you are also "renting" the sun, the beaches, the amenities and entertainment. YOU ARE RENTING A PIECE OF PARADISE, which has a huge effect on the market prices. It's not unusual to see a rise in value between 10-25% per year depending on the location, the type of real estate, and the demand.

The list as to reasons to invest in Costa Rica could go on and on, as you can find many other reasons why you should put your money in such as solid venture. But, the second part of the question-and it's important-is why should you invest now?

Back in the days when I was just a fresh immigrant to this country there was that expression in the air that sounded: "Costa Rica is a land of opportunities." Believe me, the wind still brings that call. Some opportunities have changed; some others are still the same. But all in all, Costa Rica is the most investor-friendly country, I have found in all my years traveling around the world, and I am certainly not the only one to think that way.

In our real estate terminology, Costa Rica is what we call a "baby," meaning that this market has not yet matured. In 2007, the real estate sectors in this tiny country have already gone through several generations of investors, several booms, but still, it's just the beginning. Now the large international hotel chains are coming, and both the government and private developers are spending tons of money on Costa Rica's infrastructure since tourism is about to become the number one income source to the country's coffers. Now, the local real estate markets are becoming more consistent, and prices more cohesive, as millions and millions of dollars are spent on real estate projects, marinas, world-class golf courses, as well as equestrian, shopping and surf developments.

You can bet that the next 10 to 20 years will see the emergence of a new profile of investor: the part-time investor-residents and the investor-retirees; and now is just the beginning of this new era.

So, taking into account these 12 new factual points, you might now be ready to earn a lot of money, realizing that investing in Costa Rica is going to be a very smart decision, one that you must make this year. Actually, this is going to be an ongoing financial opportunity for you and your bank account for the next millennium!

IN FEW WORDS...

There actually are many reasons why you should consider investing in Costa Rica. But just keep in mind these four main reasons:

1- Because you can: As a foreigner, you have the same legal rights as Costa Ricans when it comes to investing in real estate including full ownership, simple deed, no restrictions.

2- Because paradise is still affordable: Real estate prices are very reasonable when compared to the US and Canada.

3- Because Costa Rica is an investor-friendly country: There are no capital-gain taxes, no inheritance taxes and very low (0.25% per year) property taxes.

4- Because Costa Rica is a baby: Just beginning an unprecedented era of development and investment in the tourism and resident market.

Here is the place... Now is the time!

PART FOUR

DO YOUR HOMEWORK

DO YOUR HOMEWORK

Here is the very best tip I can give you: Before you even fly to Costa Rica, you must compile as much information as possible on the country.

After all, do you know how warm the temperature is at the beach (an average of 80°F year round)? What exactly is Rainy Season (July through October when precipitation increases) and how does it affect the roads, the basic services such as tourist support businesses or even the supermarkets, pharmacies and restaurants?

(Not much anymore). Is it absolutely necessary to speak and understand Spanish? (You can get by, but this is a Latin American country, and you would do well to know the basics, certainly if you are going to do business). How many international airports are there and which is closer to where I need to go? (Two: Juan Santamaria in San Jose in the Central Valley and near the Central Pacific beaches, and Daniel Oduber in Liberia, a short distance to the beach resort destinations of the Northwest Pacific). Do you have hurricanes? (No, Costa Rica is out of the hurricane belt). Dollars vs local currency? (Although the Costa Rican government and its banks have stabilized the *Colones*, and it is the preferred day-to-day currency, the dollar is your preferred investment currency.

Certainly, all the information you will need on Costa Rica-whether its politics, the economy, tourism, its culture, nature, and much more-is available on the internet. Of course, there are many specific guides and books written solely on this country in bookstores and online retail services.

Don't be surprised that should you check with your family, circle of friends, neighbors, or co-workers, you might find a lot of people who've visited Costa Rica lately. As we've already established, this country is an extremely popular tourist spot, so you may get some feed-back from those folks close to you, and who you really trust. Ask them what locations they liked, what they didn't, get their comment about the locals, the food, the culture and the environment. This could end up being your best source for information, completely unbiased!

Once you've gotten all this information, make a list of the areas in Costa Rica you would like to visit, and perhaps eventually make an investment. Don't forget to make a note of your researched pluses and minuses about each locale, note your comments, and prepare your questions. All of this research will be very useful in the future as you make your rounds of the nation.

Before you make the trip to Costa Rica, you will want to contact a local realtor down here online or on the phone (most of the local realtors offer toll free numbers from the United States... use them!). That's a truly great idea, because you will be able to ask, in advance, any kind of question you might have in mind before traveling. Ask the realtor if they have maps of the area, aerials, pictures, movies, and useful links. This is all part of their job to answer your questions and to address your comments. The swiftness, clarity and the detail of their answers will help you form your own opinions, and prepare a more specific investment strategy.

For example, in our company, we make 60 to 70% of our first contacts through internet queries. If we get an email, one of our agents will get back to the client immediately and help them launch their investment project in Costa Rica. Then, our other potential buyers—discounting walk-ins—use our toll-free number to get in touch with one of our agents, and the process begins the same.

We all understand that time is of the essence, and we want to make sure that when you do arrive in Costa Rica you will be prepared with the ammunition of information, and don't have to waste one second in paradise.

I remember one day, that a client walked into our office with his wife. My attention immediately focused on a large folder he was carrying under his arm. As we sat down and began our conversation about their relocation to Costa Rica, they opened the folder and they had complete, detailed research about the country, including the nature, lifestyle, tourism, etc. They knew more about Costa Rica on their first visit-this was their third day in the country-than I did after several years living down here! The couple even had all the brokers listed, region by region, with their websites, and copies of all the emails they had exchanged prior to their flight down to Central America.

After five minutes where I clarified some very specific legal details, I ran down the selection of listings that they had highlighted from their copy of our website, and we left the office for a tour of those properties. The next day, my clients were meeting with their lawyer that they had pre-selected before their trip, and two days later they were closing on an exclusive piece of property. They moved to Costa Rica a few months later.

What's most important to note here, is that this couple did their homework; they saved precious time and made the right selection immediately. Since they knew in advance the market prices and local real estate practices, they made an appropriate offer that was accepted right away by the seller. Today, their investment is worth more than double what they paid for it.

The example of this couple is not unique and in today's market the quality of your preliminary research will guarantee the success of your investment. As one of my mentors use to say back in the day, "The more time you spend planning your investment, the more money you save."

IN FEW WORDS...

Do your homework just as you would do for any other important investment. Visiting Costa Rica for the first time is a real shock to any tourist-it's a different culture with a new food and landscape, breathtaking sunsets, and of course, the best piña-coladas. While considering investing, spend some time with your agent exploring the area, the different markets, and plan your strategy based on logical and tangible reasons to buy your home away from home.

PART FIVE

BUILD YOUR TEAM

BUILD YOUR TEAM

After doing your homework, your next task will be to build your team. This is a very important phase of the process, considering this real estate investment is of paramount importance in your life. Therefore, you must insist on the highest level of professionalism, trust and competence from the people that will be entrusted with your business. After all, they will be handling very confidential information for the next few years and as your first investment in an unknown country, you want this experience to be 100% secure, while also profitable.

This last point is worth reiterating. After all, most of you already own your own home, but this venture is your first in a foreign country. Logically, you wouldn't ask for guidance on a real estate search from someone outside the area you are looking to make a fiscal investment.

No, of course not.

FIND A LOCAL REALTOR. This is the foremost priority for your team.

Your real estate agent will be guiding you through the process of purchasing a tropical retreat for your family and friends, and, of course, he will help adapt the investment strategy into reality.

What can you expect from this realtor? Experience, knowledge, and commitment.

A few more points on this subject: In Costa Rica, it is not mandatory to have a license to sell real estate nor to be registered be a real estate agent. Therefore, it would be in your best interest to find and choose a licensed realtor to do the job for you. That way, you'll have someone with an extensive knowledge of the local real estate laws and regulations, as well as access to several marketing and legal tools. The other advantage to a certified realtor is that they work with morals, principles and professionalism, generally based on the well established Code of Ethics of the United States-based National Association of Realtors®.

Going with any other real estate "specialist" option is going to be risky. Let me tell you why. You will soon find that in Costa Rica, as in many other countries, everybody appears to know about real estate, or has a good friend they know who works in real estate, or knows a friend of a friend of a cousin working in real estate. If you're lucky even your taxi driver or your street cigar salesman will show you some property for sale. You might think that they are doing this to help you, and that you will save money paying their low finder's fees instead of agent's fees. Not to mention, you might also think they will help you find a better deal.

Sure, that might be true in some cases. But, sincerely I doubt it. And in the end there is still a risk involved in going it alone when you make such an important decision investing in real estate-in Costa Rica just the same as any other country.

You must ask yourself, "Does your *contact* and new friend have a good knowledge of this country's industry laws and regulations? Have they visited the property they are selling or just seen it on the cover page of a magazine (or on a website)? Do they know if the property is titled or not? If there is a lien on it or any other limitation affecting the use of the property? Do they have access to MLS database, the multi-listing system which groups all information on properties available in each area including prices? What guarantee do they offer if something goes wrong?

I could continue with this for pages…

Surely, you need to consider what you would do if there is a problem. Where would you file a complaint? With whom?

Not too long ago, a funny thing happened to me while I was waiting for my plane at a local airport.

The aircraft was late, and I was sitting there reading a newspaper when a local street vendor approached me offering up some sodas and other refreshments. As we were having a nice conversation about the weather, he suddenly announced: "You know, I am also a real estate agent, and I have a lot of properties for sale. Do you want to see them?"

Sure I did. He was very polite and gentle. So I followed him behind the building and pulled out a file filled with papers. I immediately recognized some maps from properties in the area.

"See, I have all these properties for sale!" he continued, showing me the plans and telling me the prices. I had a closing in that town that day, and I can tell you that the prices of those properties he was hawking were two to three times the cost of other similar farms we had sold that day. Worse than that, most of the legal stamps, and signatures attesting that the plans were officially checked and registered in the national land register as well as the local municipality were missing; all the while, he was assuring me that his properties were duly registered, clear and free of liens or encumbrances.

Don't laugh; if it happened to me, it could happen to you!

So right now, without a moment's hesitation, contract a full-time, licensed realtor-not home-based-working from a real office with associates, assistants, copy machine, computers, internet, phone lines, fax and coffee machine. I say, "full time" because it takes time to get a complete knowledge of the market; it's not something you can do from home, or as a part-time job. "Licensed," because the training it takes to earn one by the local associations of real estate agents are a guarantee of legal information and ethics for you. And finally, a person working from a real office has a great source of support and resources and is duly registered with governmental and local authorities. In few words, they are for real.

I know a few "agents" working from home or on the internet, showcasing or offering listings they have never visited or are have little familiarity. And they claim to be top professionals in the real estate industry when they are just trying to capture the lead, or get a *referral fee* from an internet lead. Be on guard, in today's worldwide market boosted by sophisticated technology these are, unfortunately, current unethical practices.

Start shopping: Go online, and look into the areas you might be interested in investing. If you heard about a specific agent, *Google* his or her name and see what comes up on the internet. Eventually, talk to your friends and neighbors about your projects; they surely know somebody that has invested in Costa Rica and their feed-back will provide solid information for you. Our company often does investment seminars and participates in US and European trade shows. It is always amazing to see the level of response at the real estate fair booth or during a trade show: I would say more that 50% of the prospects we meet tell us that they've heard about Costa Rica, that their friend or a family member visited the country on vacation just a few months previously…and some of them have already experienced the benefits on investing in our tropical paradise. Amazing!

Contact the licensed real estate agents individually-via email would be the best way-and get them to answer a specific questionnaire. Don't be afraid to ask them any question you might have in mind. Go beyond the classic "So, how's business?" Instead, put forth these questions:

1. How many years have you been working in Costa Rican real estate? This "how long have you been in the business" question is very interesting and will give you an immediate and precise idea of the knowledge of your contact. An agent that has recently arrived in this country will certainly not have the same legal knowledge inventory and experience than another local broker that has been working in a specific area for a longer period of time. I like to say that a minimum of 2 years working and living full time is a good guarantee of their knowledge and experience.

2. Are you licensed by either the Costa Rica Global Association of Realtors (CRGAR) or Costa Rican Real Estate Brokers Chamber (CCCBR)? Remember that licensing is not mandatory in Costa Rica; however some local professionals decided to go through specific licensing and training sessions with the above-mentioned organizations and this is certainly proof of professionalism and a rock-solid guarantee for you.

3. Are you members of any U.S.-based real estate association such as the NAR®, or any other international real estate network? If so, you will know that they have access to constant training programs mostly on-line, and they have to stand by the NAR® Code of Ethics.

4. What is your specialty? Is it beach properties, farms, condos, commercial, hotels, or something else? I have seen so many agents specialized in... well, everything. But, believe me, selling property on the beach, and a condo in the city, a retail store in a commercial center or a farm in the inlands are different tasks. Also, each area has its own specifications and/ or regulatory urbanism plan, water associations, etc. Honestly, you can't know everything about each area. So be sure your agent is well aware of the specifics of the locale you are interested in.

5. Do you have references, a list of past clients or

contacts in your area? If they have been in business for a solid number of years, no doubt they have a client located near to where you live now. It's common policy at our company to give a list of references when requested so that you can check them out and ask them any questions related to our services and/or investing in our area. The funny thing is that most of our clients stay in touch with each other over time, and I have even seen a few of them co-investing in other projects.

6. Is real estate your full-time job? How many transactions did you close last year? Although these questions might sound a little odd, personally I just love them-especially the first one. You can't imagine how many part-time agents are working in real estate these days. How can they get a good knowledge of the inventory available or be aware of the last mortgage plan of a property if they only come to the office few hours a day? That goes for your local realtor in the US, too. You want to be sure that your agent is entirely immersed in real estate and not one of those part-time, self-employed, real estate consultants with no access to databases, or legal services. Get the agent's office information as well, so you can get feedback from the company as well.

7. Are you yourself investing in Costa Rica? For example, do you own your own home, some land, or any income producer? Ask them their own personal history, the story of how they ended up in Costa Rica, particularly the town where they are now doing business. Try to get a precise profile.

8. Do you have any specific contacts in the real estate industry that might be useful? Ask specific questions about local financing, escrow services, property management services, rental management companies, title insurance companies, etc. And, see which of the agents you speak with are the most knowledgeable and the more diligent with their responses.

9. Finally, trust your feelings and select the real estate agent that inspires in you the most confidence and respect. The first feed-back you get is generally the best. Make sure that he or she understands your needs and will be able to present you with the best opportunities on the market-the ones that suits your needs.

Let me tell you the story of an agent that came in one day and asked for a work-interview with our Tamarindo office. He was a good-looking guy, and the detail that impressed me the most is that he was very personable, the perfect buddy to have when you visit the country for the first time. He knew, of course, all the best restaurant and happy-hour bars after just few days in the area, but not a lot about local real estate laws and practices. I was thinking, "No big deal, we can still train him with a good mentor and get him his license in less that a month. And that personality is such a winner for us…"

That's what I was thinking until I asked him about his goals and motivations. And I still remember his answer: "Don't worry, I know what I am doing, and I would do anything, I mean *anything*, in order to make a commission. I will sell the listings offering the highest commissions only. Hire me and you won't regret it!"

Yes, right…

I told him that if he was getting into this business for the money, then it was the wrong reason that we were not interested in his big fat commission strategy, but rather the quality of his portfolio and his clients' satisfaction instead. He had knocked on the wrong door.

Guess what? I knew one of our competitors might be interested in his outstanding marketing skills, and I was right. Eventually, this fellow was hired by that competitor, he made few sales. Not a lot. But as promised, he was very aggressive and reported out every night at every happy-hour-at least he had some fun. He was so good that he even convinced one of his prospects-a developer-to give him the exclusive on his brand-new residential project. Needless to say, the project was poorly planned and marketed; they didn't make any sales, and it just didn't get off the ground. Eventually, the developer lost all the money he had invested in the project, as well as the land.

Today, this real estate buddy that would have done anything in order to make a commission is history. Learn from this lesson, and don't hire just any real estate agent, not even that nice guy you met at the bar the other night. You might pay the highest price for trusting him.

Another important tip: Avoid the common mistake of potential buyers, which is contracting several agents looking for the same type of property at the same time (and sometimes in the same area). Costa Rica is a small country, and these agents will sooner or later find out that they are "shopping" for the same client. If this happens, they might not take your request seriously. You don't want that when you are trying to build a trustful relationship.

Once you have a more precise profile of different agents, choose one specific agent based on the experience, record or any other positive notes or recommendations you have gathered.

And now, your choice of local real estate agent is made! Congratulations, you have a new partner in Costa Rica as well as a future neighbor and friend.

It's time to get more specific: In a few words, describe

your strategy, goals, hopes and fears.

Here's how it's done. I remember few years ago when some clients called me, and after asking the usual questions, they explained in detail that their main goal was to get their feet wet buying a two-bedroom income producer that they could use once or twice a year and rent it the rest of the year. They also said that if they were happy with the rental income, they might buy another property of this type for speculative purposes, and that their goal in the following 3-4 years was to sell in order to buy a luxury family home-something that they could not afford at the moment.

Their first investment cost them $68,000, followed the next year by another similar investment (partially paid for with the rental income of the first one) and exactly 3 years later, they sold both condos. The money from the sale of those 2 units allowed them to purchase a luxury seaside 3-bedroom townhouse they still own today. My clients are now considering selling the townhouse in order to buy a beachfront estate they have been dreaming about. Not too bad a strategy!

Another client started investing with us five years ago, and then decided to create a Private Real Estate Investment Trust (REIT) with some members of his family and friends. Today, they own an impressive portfolio of apartments, rental income producers and commercial spaces worth over $2,300,000, all from an initial investment of under $500,000.

What's their secret? Having a strategy and sticking to their goals. From the start, they have reinvested all the money generated by their rentals and the resales in projects available in the pre-construction sales stage in order to get good entry prices. Easy. And their next goal is to start developing some land in the next 2 years.

Today, our office is advising many of these Private Real Estate Investment Trusts. They are easier to manage than you think, and your agent will know how to guide you as well.

Once your own real estate strategy has been developed, is clear and cohesive, your chosen real estate agent will then connect you to some more of your needed team members. You will then add the best real estate professionals in the country including lawyers, notaries, title insurance companies, house inspectors, banks, architects, builders, interior designers, property managers, rental managers, and more.

Just as you interrogated your prospective agent, don't hesitate to ask each new professional you want to work with specific questions about the job you have in mind in order to determine which one will be the best to implement your goals. For example, you might require a lawyer specializing in real estate, but with a strong corporate law emphasis, a title insurance company that also provides escrow services, or an architect with a focus on conceiving luxury homes or condominiums, etc.

There will be just one more thing to do at this point, and that will be to get on a plane to your destination in Costa Rica and visit our tropical paradise!

IN FEW WORDS...

Building your team goes beyond selecting the first agent around the corner. Meet them personnaly and test their abilities for handling your future investment. Ask them specific questions and observe them carefully at the same time that they answer your questions. Finally, listen to your inner voice, hire the one that inspires in you the most trust and respect, and put them to work for you.

PART SIX

GET WET!

GET WET!

Congratulations, you have finally arrived in Costa Rica after a short and safe trip, have checked into your hotel and are watching a breathtaking sunset while drinking one of the best, fresh piña-coladas ever. Tomorrow you will meet your agent for the first time, go through your punch list of "Things to Do, Places to Visit and People to Meet." So, relax and enjoy your first night in paradise!

First thing in the morning after a good breakfast in front of the ocean, you will need to visit your pre-selected properties with your agent. During the trip, don't hesitate to take pictures, ask specific questions, check the general quality of the construction and the maintenance, meet the owners or the property managers administrating the place and get as much information as you need in order to assist you in the future. Don't hesitate to visit the same property twice, during day and the night time-it is always interesting to get a perspective on a property in the evening, check on its ambiance, if there are sufficient lights in the garden, enough sun around the pool in the day time and many other details you want to know in advance of closing the deal.

Eventually prepare a punch list of all the details for each property you visit and rate the property (for example 3 stars if you really like it, 2 stars if you like it but there a lots of repairs, and only one star if it's just *okay*).

While you are going through this on-site process, compare prices with similar listings in the same area and get general feed-back of the neighborhood by talking to the neighbors, tenants, business owners, etc. Ask them if they are happy about their investment, about the property manager, or any other question you might have on your mind. You will make new friends and get their valuable feed-back.

Once you have compiled all of this information, rank the properties you visited in order of preference. This is very important and will help you...develop a Plan B.

Yes, a *Plan B*, another property, a back-up to your first choice.

Why is that important?

Because you might have some problems with the sellers while negotiating the terms and conditions of the sale on your preferred choice. You might be competing with another offer from another client. You might even simply just change your mind after one night in town, because you want to avoid any kind of pressure during the purchase process.

So, having another property in back-up might be

helpful and will help you move fast with your investment project without any further frustration. or pressure.

A few years ago, a recently married couple came to Tamarindo. After a few nights, they decided that the cozy honeymooner nest-available for sale-was perfect for them, and they signed an offer to purchase. I insisted on showing them other properties knowing that, in the future, there were likely to have children, and that this first property was going to be too small for a family. I was so persistent, they ended up purchasing a 4-bedroom ocean view home…and they were still skeptical. Six years later, they have 3 kids (2 twin boys and another little girl), and they come down here at least once a year with their family and friends. Last time I saw them, I asked if they would sell their property since I had another client interested, ant their answer was that they would not sell it for anything in the world, that this home was the best investment they ever made-and they had completely forgotten about that first selection so long ago!

You would be amazed to know the number of

clients who purchase their second option. The reason is simple: Generally your first home choice is the result of a very emotional process, after all, you may be here on vacation, and if that's the case you will be impressed by the environment and dramatic sunsets (however, I must admit, after all these years, I am still impressed by both) and those will powerfully drive your emotions.

A second selection will come from one's logic, less from sentiment. Since it's a Plan B, you pay more attention to details that might make you change your decision from your first choice…and paying attention to details pays back! As you move towards your final purchase, sometimes you find out that your second property fits your needs better or simply offers more advantages than the first one.

Another case I can offer as an example is this young couple who were visiting the area and surfing the waves for the very first time. They were having so much fun in Costa Rica that they decided to invest in a small rental income producer that they themselves would be able to use a couple times per year. What they did was smart: After visiting several units, they had one of our sales associates prepare two distinct offers on two different units (but very similar in size and prices, only the owners were different).

In those days, we were in a sellers' market, and it was not really easy to negotiate due to the high demand for those specific kinds of units. Back then, we presented the offer to the owner of the unit that they liked best. Since the seller was not eager to lower his asking price, the couple wanted us to present their offer to the owner of the other unit. He accepted the proposal since he would be getting a good profit and intended to re-invest that money in a new project he wanted to get in on in the pre-sales stage.

All in all, everybody was winning, and the purchasers didn't lose their time with endless talks and negotiations. With the money the ultimately saved by that, they were able to pay for all the closing costs and personalize their new vacation home with accruements such as local tropical-style artwork. (We still see this couple around our area during New Year's and summer vacations; their surfing skills are getting better and better all the time!).

So don't neglect the importance of selecting a second property option. We all need a good Plan B!

Ultimately, once you've got your choices ready, get back to your real estate agent's office and write your offer to purchase. You are just a few steps away from owning your dream home!

IN FEW WORDS...

Get wet... the smart way. Check the property and make a punch list of the pro and cons. Eventually get another back-up property, a Plan B, in case your first offer is rejected or if you run into endless unproductive negotiations. You will know soon enough if the property you will buy is the first one that attracted you or if you should go with the back-up, which could be a better option and investment.

PART SEVEN

LOCK DOWN
THE DEAL

LOCK DOWN THE DEAL

Your work is almost done. Now, let our agent present your offer to the seller and wait for their feed-back.

In order to present your offer, he needs you to sign an Option to Purchase and Escrow Agreement, which is a document identifying the parts of the business relating to the property ID, price, payment, specifying the terms and conditions of the deal as well as the payment schedule, the identity of escrow agent, terms of escrow, and closing date, and any other details relating to that transaction. I mean ALL the details, for example, if you plan on getting local financing, don't forget to mention that in the option in order to avoid any surprises, if there is an inventory list of the furniture and equipment available at the property manager's office, print it, sign it and add it to the option, if there is a plan of the property, do the same thing...

Don't be surprised if the *Option to Purchase and Escrow Agreement* is of a simpler form than their stateside counterparts. The reason for this is that the legal system in Costa Rica is based on Civil law, permitting less interpretation by the judges; it is less complicated and shorter. In fact, the Option to Purchase and Escrow Agreement you will sign in Costa Rica will include only what the law does not already state, which is the main reason why it is less detailed than the contracts signed in the States. In any case, have your lawyer read over the contract in order to ensure that your interests are well preserved.

Also important, make this contract in English; if not,

ask your realtor to translate it into English, and when you sign, sign only this copy.

Once your realtor has redacted the contract and you have signed it, he will now present the offer to the seller.

You basically will be confronted with three responses:

1. THEY WILL REJECT YOUR OFFER.

This might happen in some cases, such as when you are purchasing in the pre-construction phase and you already have the benefit of getting a unit under market value-sometimes 20-25% under its real worth. (That's why it's smart to be investing at this stage.) If the developer is not under pressure, he will stand firm at his price. However, in some specific cases-for example, if you buy several units at the same time-you might get some kind of discount by investing in pre-sales stage.

One tip: If you can't get a discount, try for another advantage not within the selling price, such as upgrades in finishings, a better payment plan, etc.

Getting your offer rejected is not necessarily a bad sign, it shows that the listing you want to purchase has solid good value on the market, and eventually, there are lots of potential future buyers who will have interest in it. You will appreciate that the day you re-sell the property. In any case, if the seller rejects your offer, don't be offended, ask your agent what the reasons were that the offer was rejected, analyze his feed-back and ultimately, change your offer.

If, in fact, you don't want to move from your first offer, this is the time to go to your Plan B, and present the offer on the second listing that caught your attention. It might be the one you end-up buying!

2. YOU GET A COUNTER-OFFER FROM THE SELLER.

The second option you receive is a counter-offer from the seller, after all, this is a negotiation process… so be patient. This means your first offer was too low, but it also means that the seller is still very interested in your bid. In that case, you still want to get as much information as you can in order to negotiate the best deal. So get back to your agent. Since he was in direct contact with the seller, he generally knows the reasons and the math the seller did in order to present the counter-offer, and what space is left for the negotiation. Your broker's feed-back will be important and is going to save you time and money.

One other tip: Don't try to over-negotiate and systematically "counter the counter offer."

I remember a case like this when one of my clients was trying to purchase a rental income producer. His first offer was low, but the seller decided to counter-offer what I thought was a fair price and still a good deal for the purchaser. Then my client tried to get a furniture package included, which resulted in upsetting the seller. Ultimately, he decided not to sell his condo to the purchaser. End of the game.

Negotiating is a very sensitive phase, act wisely.

3. YOUR OFFER IS ACCEPTED

The best news of all is when you learn that your offer is accepted. That means you've made a smart move, and you've won. Congratulations!

With your agent, contact your lawyer, prepare your wire transfer, and celebrate. Have a good dinner with your family and friends, a bottle of premium local rum, a sunset cruise. (Why not? It's fun!)

You are now just few steps away to owning your new Home away from Home...

IN FEW WORDS...

Closing the deal is all about details and negotiation skills. The details are those that you want mentioned in the contract of Option to Purchase, the document that is the basis of the final deed you will sign at the lawyers. It will mention ALL the terms and conditions of the transactions. You will need your negotiation skills in order to get that offer accepted by the seller. Don't be shy, but be fair, realistic and respectful about the other part involved in the transaction.

PART EIGHT

PREPARE

THE CLOSING

PREPARE THE CLOSING

Generally, you will get 30-45 days to close the deal, sometimes longer. For example, in the case we discussed, where you purchase in pre-sales stage, you might get 6-9 months before you are required to begin payments.

Your realtor will prepare the closing with you and your lawyer, which means that both of them will go through all the specifics outlined in the Option to Purchase and Escrow Agreement. The lawyer on your side will process a due diligence which includes:

1. Doing a title study at the *Registro Nacional* (Costa Rica Land Registry), checking on current and past property owners. Checking the area of the property to see if it matches what you have been told. Checking if the property is free and clear of any lien or encumbrance.

2. Also checking if the property plans are duly stamped and registered with the *Cadastro Nacional*, (Land Register), the *Colegio de Ingenieros y Topografos*, and is some case the Municipality, depending if you purchase a condominium, some raw land or a lot in a gated community.

3. Determining if the property is owned by a corporation. In that case, your lawyer will have to request the corporation books and make a complete study about it including whether the corporation is up-to-date on its tax payments.

4. Issuing a last-minute study, to ensure you more security during the last days before your closing in case of the discovery of anything affecting the title itself or the use of the property.

5. Consulting several national agencies such as the Ministry of the Environment, Ministry of Taxation, and your local Municipality to make sure that property taxes are paid up to date; as well as private companies, such as the homeowner association to make sure that the fees are paid up to date and there are no restrictions affecting the use of the property you are purchasing; the property manager to make sure that the maintenance and fees are paid to date, that no big expenses are planned or coming up, that the insurance is paid, and that an inventory has been made of what's inside the house; and the rental agent in order to have an exhaustive detail of all the upcoming rentals and prepared deposits for future tenants in order to deduct that from the future selling price to make sure the accounting is square before you go to the closing.

6. Preparing with the realtor the coordination of two property inspections-the first one just after signing the Option, in order to check it to see if there are any potential hazards that will effect the immediate use of the property; and then another inspection just before

the Closing to ensure that repairs have been completed and that everything else on the site is okay.

Preparing your closing also means preparing your payments. Don't forget that time is of the essence and that any delays in the transfer of funds might affect the closing. Generally, our advice is that you should wire the necessary closing funds to your escrow agent a minimum 10 days prior to the closing in order to avoid last minutes surprises, addendums and negotiations.

Also, avoid another common mistake, which is getting surprised by the closing fees. Ask your agent and your lawyer to let you know in advance what the exact amount of the closing fees and other expenses related to the transaction are going to be in order to add this amount into your money transfer.

Your real estate agent will send you constant reports so that you can oversee (and control) the entire process during the countdown to the closing.

In conclusion, to prepare your closing means to anticipate your needs, and that includes those that will come up when you eventually arrive in Costa Rica. Those requirements include the opening of a local bank account (the only document you'll need is your passport), purchasing any items in order to personalize your property to your own taste or to make it more comfortable, and contacting all the future partners that will be involved in helping you with your new home (architects, interior designers, property managers, vacation rental agents, contractors, etc.).

And, most important of all, since you will soon own a vacation home in a Latin America tropical paradise, practice your Spanish!

IN FEW WORDS...

Preparing the closing is the basic process of due diligence of the property you are planning to purchase. At this point, your lawyer and your real estate agent will work together based on the information they already have and the public and private information available about the property. This stage is very technical and will result in the drafted deed that you will sign at closing. So get a good lawyer, and make sure to that your real estate agent keeps you informed each step of the due diligence. Prepare your payment, and any other formality related to your transaction now.

PART NINE

D-DAY

D-DAY

Here you are: Your funds are in Costa Rica and you will close tomorrow.

Don't forget to visit the property one last time prior to the closing to see if there is any detail that catches your attention, such as a leak, or any malfunction that might not have been fixed at your request. If needed, take some digital pictures. There will still be an opportunity to make a comment at the closing in order to get a commitment from the seller or any other arrangement.

In some cases, buyers may not be present at the closing-it happens more often that you think and you can actually have a third part signing on your behalf using a Power of Attorney. One of our best clients-an investor who comes to Costa Rica a couple of times per year-often jokes that he is never here when he presents offers and/or closes his deals. He's not really kidding: So far, he has purchased and sold over than 12 properties, and was only present at 2 closings.

What we do for our clients who are not here in person, is go to the site on their behalf in order to perform our client's property inspection. If needed, we take photographs, and prepare a punch list with details to be fixed. These documents are then sent to their lawyer, and since we are at the closing, we discuss these issues directly with the seller before we sign the deal. In case there is an important repair to be done, or in case property taxes and/or the owner's association fees haven't been paid by the seller prior to closing, it is possible to still sign the deed and leave part of the payment (corresponding to the sums needed) in escrow with the attorney. These funds will be released to the seller as soon as the problem is fixed, or your lawyer will pay the taxes and fees directly from these funds kept in escrow. This procedure shows that you are flexible, and generally everything gets solved very quickly.

The last step is for you to sign the deed… don't forget that document will be written in Spanish and make sure you get it translated before the moment you sign it. It could be a verbal translation, but we prefer a written translation on a separate document and in some cases certified by a translator registered with your embassy.

Once everything is clear, just sign the deed and process the payments.

You are now the happy owner of a charming tropical retreat, a rental income producer, or you've got the vacation home of your dreams.

Welcome to the neighborhood!

IN FEW WORDS...

What is there to say about the closing day except that it has to be a happy day... a perfect day...! However, don't forget one important thing: The deed you will sign will be in Spanish, so make sure that your lawyer prepares a translation of the deed into English to be reviewed before signing in order to get a complete and detailed understanding of the document.

PART TEN

BEYOND

THE CLOSING

BEYOND THE CLOSING

Pura Vida! It's now time to enjoy your investment; it's also time to assume your duties as a new owner. My best advice is to find a way, as fast as possible, to spend one night in your new home so you can feel its ambiance. After that, begin meeting all your new business partners and move on with your rental-management strategy, remodeling project, and maintenance plan.

A good property management company and/or a good rental agent could make a huge difference on your return on your investment. However, just like your precautions in choosing a real estate agent, you must be wise in picking this part of your team.

As to your rental agent, try to get a complete and detailed list of the marketing tools they would use, and the typical results they get. Also ask for recommendations and references. Finally, compare their prices with the other companies you are interviewing, and then make your decision. Keep in mind that the cheapest alternative might not be the best one. Bottom line is that you want top-quality management and rental-marketing people that will get results and help you improve your income.

I usually get my clients to select the best property managers operating in the area or the best rental agents. I think that the price or the fees they get is less an issue than the quality of the service they provide and the marketing they do in order to maintain your unit in good shape, and get it rented as many weeks as possible to well-qualified tenants. I don't think I would personally be ready to put my vacation home in the hands of just *any* manager, and I guess you would probably feel the same way.

On the other hand, the rental market is very competitive in Costa Rica, and you want to be sure your rental agent will be able to provide you with the best marketing tools in order to get a good income and not just enough to cover the maintenance fees. So balance out these factors when making your choice.

Most clients, when they come to the area, sign a contract with a large property management/rental company, which could be a **BIG** mistake-one that could end up effecting their pocketbook. Most of these big companies, when they are well organized, have a large inventory of apartments, with a limited number of requests for those units, when a client comes in to rent, they might not lease out your condo, sidestepping your financial goals. It's a roll of the dice, so to speak. As a matter of fact, we hear a lot of our own clients tell us they prefer independent vacation rental agents, who focus only on marketing and managing only few units in order to generate a better income.

Choose the best property manager using these

criteria: cost control for your unit; quality maintenance; sidestep the less expensive one for the one you want to work with; and then choose a separate rental management that is going to offer you the best marketing strategy, and fill your unit with vacationers as often as possible. Also, ask around for some information about the manager from local residents or tenants, and you will quickly become aware of their strengths and weaknesses.

One last tip: Regarding the rental, be sure that you will be allowed to rent the unit to people you know, when you want to, without too much of an extra percentage paid out to your property manager (or just a flat key-fee to the company in charge of performing the check-in and check-out).

I would suggest you simply have a business meeting with your property manager and your rental manager in order to fix your goals for the first 2-3 years. Get their feed-back and plan the strategy that makes the most sense.

If your new purchase is a lot or a farm, visit the

property at different times of the day. Go at the point of sunset, and try to check the sun exposure, dominant winds, identify in detail the fauna and flora, because you or your architect might need all that information in the future.

Whatever the property, it's always a good idea to meet the neighbors and make new friends. They will be a great source of information giving you many useful tips.

One very important final recommendation: Stay in touch with your real estate agent, your lawyer and the original seller. You never know when you might need their help at any moment in the future. During this entire process, you have built a trusting and friendly relationship with some of the best real estate professionals in Costa Rica. You shared with them and affection for this beautiful country, and a common vision on an investment strategy for yourself.

This very exclusive relationship is a major key to your future investments. All statistics show that the same real estate agent is generally able to sell and resell the same property several times; therefore, he will be a key business partner the day you decide to resell your property, he might even tell you when you should re-sell and for how much. Let him know your plans, it could be as simple as saying, "Call me when my property is worth xx-amount of dollars on the market," and it generally works.

In case you plan on purchasing more properties in the future, your personal real estate agent is already familiar with your taste, knows your goals and negotiating skills. He will save you precious time and money on your next real estate deal.   He might even have a client that will make you an offer.

Most of our clients became our friends over the years. We stay in touch, exchange information and we don't miss one "excuse" to go surfing or golfing together when they are in the area. To tell you the truth, we tend to share more personal news about our kids, that new, exciting restaurant that opened in town, the size of the waves and the breathtaking sunsets than professional information in our last real estate newsletter. But, I guess that is the sign of strong and friendly relationships, and I like it this way.

IN FEW WORDS...

Beyond the closing is when your entire strategy makes sense. Now's the time to put all percentages on your side and improve the curb appeal of your property by making any upgrade-if necessary-and signing a contract with the best property managers and rental agents. This will assist in maximizing your investment.

Also, stay in touch with your real estate agent: He or she is your connection to the local real estate market you just invested in and will keep you informed at any time of more of the best opportunities for you.

PART ELEVEN

BUYING ONLINE

BUYING ONLINE

More and more clients every day are buying properties online. It's quite a natural thing when you consider that 60-70% of our leads come through the internet, but still it's quite a new buying trend in the third millennium of the real estate industry.

This practice is common, and a direct consequence of the influx in new technologies. Generally, online buyers are motivated by the opportunity of getting to invest in Costa Rica before they plan a trip to visit. Therefore, as soon as a decision is made, an agent will send them the reservation contract or the option to purchase, to be signed by both them and the seller. After that, they just have to wire the deposit down to the local escrow agent.

There is no specific risk in using the online strategy of buying. We are doing it every day at each of our offices. We also happen to sign reservation contracts while we are attending trade shows outside of Costa Rica, and both will be important ways of selling-and buying-real estate in the future.

Why is that?

Primarily because today's market moves fast. Let's face it: Technology allows sellers-at low cost-to present and feature properties worldwide on the internet, and therefore allow access to a larger market which, of course, increases the chances of getting offers. Under these circumstances, if you wait too long there is a good chance the listing you want will be sold before you travel to Costa Rica. That's why more and more of our clients opt for the alternative of purchasing online and at least signing the Option before they get to the country. Once you sign the Option, it generally takes 30-45 days to close which gives you enough time to come and visit the property in person.

I would say that today more than 50% of the deals we sign are closed online, at trade shows or seminars. The main reason is that our prospects trust our name and experience, we have strong references in that field and we pre-qualify all the projects we are selling, as well as the developers, in order to feature only rock solid ventures and quality listings.

By purchasing online you make faster moves and increase your opportunities and chances for profits. It's a fact.

Again there is no risk involved in this practice as long as you know what you are doing and who you are dealing with. By this stage in reading of the book, you already know the exact mistakes to avoid and the strategy to plan in order to make a safe investment.

So, if you decide to invest online there are few things you need to know:

1-   Stick to your goals and methodology, and select only the real estate agents that will answer your specific needs and will give you all the guarantees and references required. You already know how to proceed if you have been reading the previous chapters. So, don't try to skip any of the phases we mentioned in this book. Keep on doing your homework, building your team, preparing your offer, etc. It will just take few emails and conversations with your agent to get through these details and secure your investment.

2-   Avoid a big mistake: Going it alone and buying directly online from a developer or a seller. You might be lucky at this game or you might end up purchasing over market value, or not adapting your long-term investment plans; when you realize this, it will be too late. Remember a developer or an owner will never give you comparables from the area, will try to get you to use their lawyer, and will not necessary help you negotiating the offer…that's your agent's job and responsibility.

3- Buying online does mean a little more work and methodology when it comes to choosing the professionals and services related to your transaction- lawyer, escrow agent, title insurance company, mortgage broker, interior designer, property manager, rental manager, etc. So first, put your agent to work for you and be sure you are provided with several options and names in each category in order to base your selections on different alternatives and references.

For example, we work with several law firms all specializing in corporate law and real estate deals, but we already know which one will be indicated for a commercial transaction, for a real estate development, or for a specific zone or small, mid or large-size deal.

We also know which property manager will be good for a condo project, and which other one will be better for a luxury home.

When it comes to financing your purchase with a local or US bank, we have the best connections and will direct you to the most appropriate institutions.

As stated in this book, it's not only about making the deal happen, but also about making it easy, fast and secure. Simply put, using our knowledge and experience to your advantage in order to help you save precious time and money when planning your investment in or relocation to our little piece of paradise.

IN FEW WORDS...

Buying online or out of the office happens... more than you might think. There is nothing wrong or risky about this procedure when you follow the guidelines and tips mentioned in here in this book. Just be sure you are represented and assisted by a qualified and renowned real estate agent and all will be successful. You might even save precious time and get your deal closed quickly, in the safest way, which is an opportunity you can't pass on. Just stick to your goals and your strategy.

PART TWELVE

CONCLUSION

CONCLUSION

Purchasing a property in Costa Rica can be a very rewarding and life changing experience, as long as it is well planned and done the right way. This book is the result of 23 years experience in the real estate industry of which the last 11 years were dedicated to selling real estate in Costa Rica. I hope these lines gave you a simple, friendly and clear, general overview in order to get the process of buying your tropical home easier, faster and secure.

One of my best clients and friends once said that the

only mistake he ever made when he started investing in Costa Rica was…not buying more real estate. Today, he is still here, buying and selling properties, having started with a very reasonable investment, his portfolio now includes the creation of two private real estate investment trusts (one with his family, one other with private partners), as well as a company investing in rental income producers. These facts, and what I've laid out in this book are the best arguments to convince you to invest in Costa Rica and that your slice of paradise is waiting for YOU!

The real estate buying process in Costa Rica need not be intimidating or confusing, and I believe that in understanding the steps in the process and pitfalls to avoid, a buyer can make the right moves and enjoy their investment for years to come.

And finally, remember that Costa Rica is still what we call a baby, a merging real estate market with a great future and tons of opportunities for the wise investors.

Do not hesitate to contact me if you have any doubts, any comment or question, or if you would like any more specific information.

Best yet, come down and see us here. I look forward to meeting you soon in our little piece of paradise where I live happily in Playa Tamarindo with my lovely wife, our two little girls and our dog and cats.

Pura Vida!

12 MOST FREQUENTLY ASKED QUESTIONS

And My Answers and Tips

12 MOST FREQUENTLY ASKED

QUESTIONS

1- Is Costa Rica really a secure country to invest in when you are a foreigner and when you are not a resident?

It certainly is a secure place when considering investing in Central America, and to my knowledge it might be the safest. There are several reasons for that. First of all, there's the stability of the government and the democracy in the country, the oldest democracy in Central America. Then I would point out the fact that real estate ownership-simple deed, fully titled-is guaranteed by the Constitution, even for foreigners, non-residents in the country. All of the information is centralized and recorded in the Registro Nacional (land registry). Finally, I would say that the fact the main title insurance companies, the names people from North American are familiar with, are represented in the country is a signal of the strength of the legal system when it comes to owning real estate in this tropical paradise.

2- *What is the best way to invest, individually or through a shelf corporation?*

Whatever works best for you according to your planned strategy. Actually, buying or owning property through a shelf corporation offers various advantages, the main one being lower transfer fees (1.25% total instead of 4%), which represents a significant saving especially if you are purchasing or selling a luxury property. Another advantage of owning your property through a corporation is that you can easily involve new investors, partners or members of your family in your ownership just by transferring them shares. It might happen that the property you want to purchase is already pre-owned by a shelf corporation; in that case the transfer of property happens by transferring the shares of the corporation to yourself and eventually your partners. I have no problem with that as long as your lawyer makes a complete due diligence of the existing corporation you are about to get.

3- Is it necessary to open a bank account in the country when investing? How long does it take to transfer funds from the US?

This is highly recommended, especially if you are going to receive a regular rental income. Opening a bank account generally takes no more than an hour and a first deposit. You can open an account in US dollars, euros, or colones–the local currency. This account can be opened in your own name, or your corporation's name, and you can get various related services from the bank such as online account access, checking, major credit cards or loans. It generally takes 2-3 days to transfer funds (swift transfer) from the US or Europe, but be sure you have all the correct wire transfer information as well as the complete name of the final beneficiary. If there is any mistake in your transfer receipt, the money will be wired back into your bank account and you will have to begin the procedure again, losing precious time. My advice is: From the moment you know the approximate closing date, select an escrow agent (most of the title insurance companies and the notaries offer that service) and send the funds to that escrow agent (even if it is one month prior to closing date) with the instruction to disburse them to the final beneficiary only at closing.

4- Is it absolutely necessary to use the services of a title insurance company when investing in Costa Rica?

It's not mandatory, but I highly recommend it to my clients, my family and best friends. Most people will tell you that it's not necessary, but if it is your first purchase in a foreign country and if the service is available…why not use it? You might also think that it is an extra expense and you might think you don't need it, but will soon discover that title insurance companies also offer full packages of various real estate-related services at no extra cost.

5- *What about financing?*

You can easily finance your purchase in Costa Rica using some US-based mortgage companies and financial institutions. You can also use your IRA account. But, in most cases, the easiest and fastest way to proceed will be to go through a local bank or mortgage broker. We have a partnership with the largest mortgage company in Costa Rica, and every week, we assist several of our clients in getting local financing. The loan to value (LTV) is 70-80% of the purchased price. The interest rate in US dollars is close to the interest rates of a second home purchase in the United States, and the only collateral needed is your down payment and a lean on the property itself. Of course, your credit record and annual income will be important, and this information will be checked by the local bank.

6- *How, where and when do I have to pay my yearly property taxes?*

We are talking about the 0.25% tax on the declared-assesed value of your property. That tax has to be paid to the Municipality every year in January for the whole year. It can be done by your property manager or your lawyer and they will generally have to go onsite make the payment and get a receipt. Don't forget to ask them for a copy of that receipt and keep tracking that the payment is made on time, otherwise you will have to pay penalties.

7- *Do I need to insure my property?*

Yes, insurance against fire, water damages and natural risks is highly recommended and is some case mandatory (if you own a condominium, for example). After that, insurance against robbery is optional and depends on the risk you anticipate (i.e., living in a gated community where 24/7 security reduces the risks of robbery), and also the belongings you want to protect. Insurance in Costa Rica is a state monopoly and as a result of that very inexpensive compared to the rates in the US. Again your property manager, your real estate agent or your lawyer will guide you through that process and help you choose the best alternative.

8- *How do I furnish and equip my place?*

In some cases, your new tropical retreat may come already furnished and equipped; in some others, it may not or simply might not meet your expectations or your personal taste. No worries, you will find a lot of reputable interior designers willing to help you with the tasks of furnishing, outfitting and decorating your place, not to mention some large furnishing companies are offering in-house interior designer services—free-of-charge—if you buy from them. Have fun and don't hesitate to go tropical, Zen, modern, or any other style. Your agent should easily provide you with a list of local professionals that will meet your budget.

9- *What are the best months of the year for renting my property?*

High season (dry season) starts early December and finishes end of April. These months are the busiest and the most expensive when it comes to renting a property. July and August are also considered as high season months as well. However, we have been observing that some destinations within Costa Rica are more in demand than others and consequently are busy all year around except a few months out of the year (September to November) during the green (rainy) season. So, if potential rental income is part of your investment strategy, your homework will be to check out which are the hottest vacation destinations in the country. Again your agent should help with this, but I will give you a clue: Generally the beach towns with large commercial and tourism infrastructure (commercial centers, supermarkets, tour companies, restaurants, bars, clubs, marina, local airport, etc.) are the signposts of high, near-year-round tourism activity.

10- Do I have to be in Costa Rica when reselling my property?

No, your presence is not required as long as you can get somebody to represent you at the closing and sign the deed on your behalf using an appropriate, certificated Power of Attorney. The money will be immediately transferred into your account and based on your previous instructions by the escrow agent, and a copy of the deposit or the transfer will be provided. However, you might want to be present at closing in order to check any last-minute details, meet your purchaser or reinvest your money in another smart transaction using your experience and knowledge.

If you can't be there at closing-whether you are selling or purchasing the property-it won't be a problem.

11- I heard that lack of infrastructure is an issue, is that true?

Yes and no. The boom of tourism and its effect on the real estate industry in Costa Rica is very recent. Subsequently, the country and the local communities are way behind with the development of the local infrastructure: expansion of the San Jose and Liberia international airports, improvement of the local domestic airports, upgrading and pavement of the roads in general, rains water collection system and black water treatment plants, urbanism planning and equipment, etc. That being said, the government itself and its institutions, the Municipalities and the local associations of residents and developers are well aware of the emergency to prepare the country for the massive tourism boom bursting through our door, and several projects are in process or will be started shortly, boosted by public and private funds. It's clear now that Costa Rica will be the #1 vacation destination in Central America and it looks like there is a general consensus between government and private partners in order to improve the infrastructure and at the same time to preserve the natural beauty of this tropical paradise. So don't be afraid or shocked if you visit a beach town featuring lots of construction projects going on as well as poor infrastructure, its part of transition taking place as the country grows up fast. Talk to your agent and get any information related to the agenda of the local infrastructure improvements. You will soon discover that local developers, business owners and residents are all working these issues. My best advice is to be patient and try to project yourself in the future, anticipate how the town will look once the infrastructure is completed, and what its effect will be on your initial investment.

12- *How do you think the market is going to evolve in the next 5-10 years, and is it still the right moment to invest?*

First, if you have access to specific information and knowledge, it is always the right moment to invest.

Remember that Costa Rica is a land of opportunities for the savvy investor and that these opportunities are numerous. Over the years, some of our clients have been investing in condos or vacation homes, but also in large farms or individual lots situated within local gated communities, commercial retail stores and storage bodegas, restaurants, small hotels, bed & breakfasts, and even reforested teak farms or marina docks. Regarding the market and its potential, keep in mind that Costa Rica is a unique vacation destination and that at the moment large international hotel chains and development groups are investing hundreds of millions of US dollars in the country.

To put it briefly, and as previously stated in this book, Costa Rica is just at the beginning of what will be a major boom of tourism and investment, a factor of unprecedented increase in wealth and opportunities for the entire country. Now is the time, here is the place, today even more than yesterday.

ABOUT US

CENTURY 21

Coastal Estates

The #1 Real Estate Network in Costa Rica

About CENTURY 21 Coastal Estates

Steadily growing along with international interest in Costa Rica real estate, the CENTURY 21 network of offices and real estate professionals is currently the largest in Costa Rica. Located on the beautiful Gold Coast in Costa Rica's Guanacaste province, our experienced team of real estate agents has been drawn here from all over the world including the US and Europe. Our licensed brokers and agents are connected to the best real estate professionals: lawyers, mortgage brokers, architects, property managers, rental agents, and interior designers.

The #1 Real Estate Network in Costa Rica

In business since 1975, CENTURY 21 Coastal Estates understands that relocating or purchasing a vacation property in a foreign country is not an easy job. Moving to Costa Rica and doing business abroad requires a great deal of research, trust and reliance on your local real estate experts. At CENTURY 21 Coastal Estates, we are committed to providing you with that trustworthy assistance every step of the way.

Recognized as Costa Rica's beach property specialists, CENTURY 21 Coastal Estates is the only real estate company in Costa Rica serving over 10 locations: Playa Tamarindo, Playa Grande, Playa Langosta, Playa Conchal, Playa Brasilito, Playa Flamingo, Playa Avellanas, Playa Negra, the Papagayo Gulf, Playa Herradura in the central Pacific, and San Jose, as well as many other "secret spots" located along the Pacific coast.

Whether your dream is to invest in a beachfront

villa, an ocean view home, a rental income producer or to simply purchase a vacation home for your family and friends, we will do our best for you.

For more information you can visit our website at
www.costarica1realestate.com
email us at info@coastalestate.org or
contact us at

011 (506) 2653-0300

or

1-866-978-6585 from US and Canada.

TESTIMONIALS
FROM OUR CLIENTS

THEIR TRUE STORIES,
TIPS AND ADVICES

Tom KRIZ, Connecticut 2007

"My wife and I fell in love with Costa Rica in 1992 when we went there on our honeymoon. We stayed in a beautiful hotel on the beach and enjoyed the local people and the surrounding area. The following year, we simply traveled around the country staying wherever we were that afternoon. We found amazing places in Arenal for $18 per night including breakfast, and $20 for a cabin directly on the beach in Playa Hermosa. Subsequent years, we rented homes for a month or more, as we had a daughter and found it was much easier to have a fixed location.

"In 1999, we realized how much we enjoyed Costa Rica and agreed that we should look to purchase a place of our own. Although we had never stayed overnight in Tamarindo, we often visited because of the great beach, surf, many restaurants and friendly people. Since it was a thriving town, it offered many more amenities then other beach areas. We decided on a condo because

of the ease of maintenance, security and rental opportunities. Relying on several recommendations, we purchased our home sight unseen over the internet. We furnished it and were totally satisfied when we finally made our first visit several months later. Throughout the process, our local real estate agent was there to help where needed. Our home has been essentially self sustaining since we purchased it.

"Recognizing the growth in the area, I was offered an opportunity to purchase commercial property across from the beach at a very attractive price. At the time, I was looking for ways to diversify my IRA holdings which were then invested primarily in equity stocks. Working with a company in the US, I established a trust which was then funded with my IRA dollars. These funds were then used to purchase the store. Income generated from the rental of the store is kept on a tax-free basis as the revenue stays within the trust until withdrawn. Values have continued to increase as Tamarindo continues to grow and expand.

"In 2006, a group of like-minded friends decided that we should look for a parcel of land that could be developed and at the same time be close enough to Tamarindo to take advantage of the entertainment, restaurants and shopping. As a result we *purchased 2-1/2 hectares in nearby Playa Avellanas. Here again, we are looking to take advantage of the continued growth and opportunities in the Tamarindo area."*

Peter and Marie <u>KURBIKOFF</u>, Nevada 2007

"Five years ago, I retired from a Fortune 500 company in San Diego, and my wife and I purchased a lovely home in Las Vegas. Since we loved to travel throughout the world, we booked a vacation trip to Costa Rica after hearing so much about this country from friends and relatives.

"It truly takes a visit to appreciate the natural beauty of Costa Rica, its culture, and the friendliness of its people. My wife and I immediately fell in love with Costa Rica on that first trip, so we have decided to purchase a piece of property and build a dream house in the beautiful coastal province of Guanacaste, in the vicinity of the town of Tamarindo.

"At first we were apprehensive about our investment since we had no idea about this country's real estate practices and the country's rules and regulations regarding foreign investors. In the States, we take these things almost for granted. Some of our concerns covered: Finding a reliable real estate agency, escrow company,

title search, title insurance, closing fees, property registration, etc. We quickly and pleasantly discovered that the system used in Costa Rica is paralleled by the system used in the United States. Furthermore, key US. companies have branches/subsidiaries in Costa Rica bearing the parent companies' name. Other benefits we discovered included the fact that Costa Rica offers unique real estate advantages such as low real estate taxes and no capital gain taxes for non-corporate investors, not to mention that the prices were from far less expensive than where we live or were use to investing in the US For the same investment, we would basically be able to get 2 or 3 times what we would get in the US!

"So, by the time we finished our market research, it was obvious for us that we were going to retire and invest in Costa Rica.

"During our first trip, we purchased our first property using the professional services of CENTURY 21 Coastal Estates and used Stewart Title as our escrow company. A year later, we purchased a second property for investment purposes, and shortly thereafter we purchased two additional properties, also for investment purposes.

"We are pleased with the ease of the investments we made. They are appreciating rapidly in value. We are looking forward

to sharing our retirement time between our house in Las Vegas and our tropical retreat in Costa Rica."

<u>Mike McCARTNEY</u>, California 2007

"In the late 1990s, my wife and I began considering investing in a vacation home abroad for our family. As we are Southern Californians who live in a beach community, we wanted to look at warmer climates near the beach without the congestion and massive overdevelopment we have seen in many otherwise pristine locales.

"My wife began reading about various locations, and Costa Rica was written about as a friendly, beautiful country with opportunities for investment. We spoke to several people who had visited Costa Rica and a few who owned property. The only thing left was to visit Costa Rica.

"Our search focused on the Playa Tamarindo area. It was described as a 'little piece of paradise' surrounded by a large nature preserve. At that time, travel to Tamarindo was mainly by small aircraft or driving (on roads of varying quality) from San Jose. Our first impression of Tamarindo was of a quiet, small

fishing village situated off the middle of a beautiful coastline. There were shady palm trees, small restaurants offering great food and friendly Costa Ricans (Ticos). In addition, there was a cosmopolitan atmosphere, with many of the businesses owned by people from around the world. We had no language barrier as English was spoken everywhere.

"After exploring the town, we sought input from several North Americans who lived year-round in the area. We connected with a very reputable real estate office and were shown various properties. Most valuable was the information they gave regarding investing in Costa Rica: a lot to know!

"Our biggest concerns were:

"(1) Who will look after our property when we are not there?

"(2) Is there a rental market?

"(3) Can we find a good agent to manage our property?

"Those questions were answered to our satisfaction, and we took the leap and purchased a new 2-bedroom condo about 5 minutes from the ocean.

"Since that time, we have vacationed 2-3 times a year with our family and many friends. The improved infrastructure in, and

around Tamarindo, has made the town even more popular with foreign tourists. We found a very effective property management firm that looks after our home when we are away. By working with travel agencies worldwide, they find tenants for our home and have provided us with a regular source of rental income since our purchase. The rental dollars from our property has always provided more than enough income to cover expenses and plenty for us.

"Beyond our practical concerns when we purchased our property, we couldn't have had so much fun without many of the people we've known. Our children quickly began feeling that Tamarindo was their second home. It's hard to come HOME after enjoying the surf, food, sun and laid back atmosphere in Costa Rica.

"As the area has grown, so has the property value of our investment. We are quite happy with this aspect. Our advice to potential investors is to know what and why you want to invest in Costa Rica, and, if you decide to go ahead, deal with established professionals who have ALL the answers."

Tim and Roseanne SMITH, New York 2007

"Having traveled to Costa Rica for the last five years, we knew *it was time to buy. It was the best move we ever made: personally and financially!*

"Our 'real estate journey' started with a visit to the local real estate office, as they offered American name recognition through their Century 21 affiliation. They were also the oldest real estate firm in Tamarindo, and they were the largest. Their expertise, knowledge and experience in the Tamarindo area was invaluable in helping us find just the right property to meet our needs, making the whole buying process a smooth, enjoyable experience from start to finish-from finding the property, selecting a lawyer, setting up bank accounts and even moving in. They cared about us as people, but then, that is what Costa Rica is all about.

"Having purchased our condo at the start of the real estate boom, we have certainly enjoyed watching it appreciate while we share it with family and friends (and we also enjoy the rental income when we're back in the States), but that is not what makes Costa Rica so great. The essence of Costa Rica lies in its raw, yet naturally powerful beauty; it's exotic and bio-diverse nature. Where else can you eat so well for so little, surf, fish, and dive, or explore nature, all in the same day? Add to that a people who still value family as much as hard work and it is like going back

in time to a kinder and gentler existence.

"It is no wonder that more and more retirees are calling Costa Rica 'home,' and why not? As the locals like to say: 'Pura Vida... To the good life.'

"And to our local real estate agent we have you to thank for helping us realize our dream!"

COSTA RICA

Maps

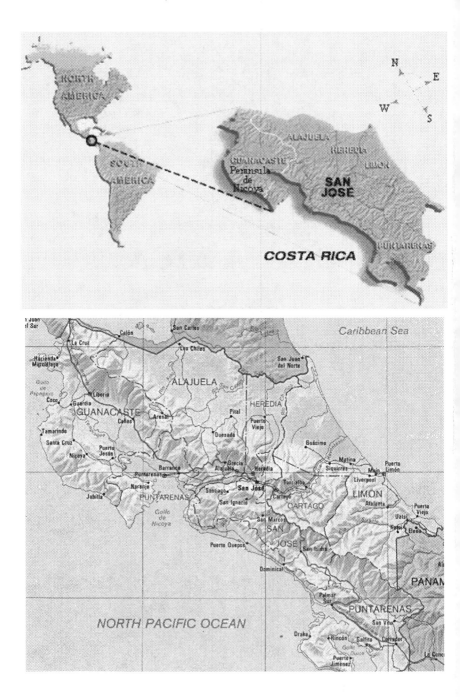

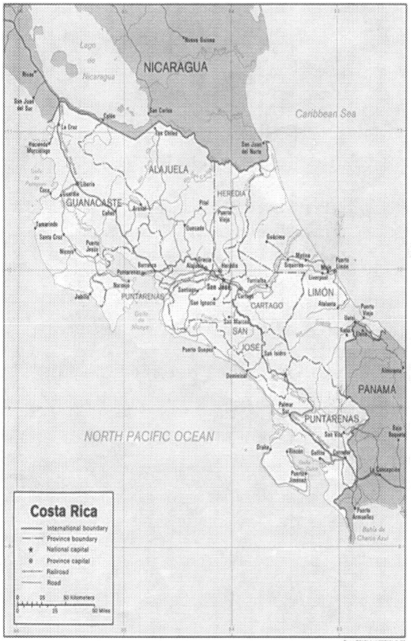

To contact Nicholas Viale:

CENTURY 21 Coastal Estates
Playa Tamarindo – Costa Rica
Central America

Phone: 011(506) 2653-0300
Fax: 011(506) 2653-0600

Call free from the US: 1-866-978-6585

Email
Realtor506@aol.com

For more information about us
and our listings

Visit our Website:
www.CostaRica1RealEstate.com

To attend our investment seminars
in Costa Rica, the United States
Canada and Europe

Go to:

www.InvestinCostaRicaSeminars.com